Paddling Alaska

Help Us Keep This Guide Up to Date

Every effort has been made by the author and editors to make this guide as accurate and useful as possible. However, many things can change after a guide is published—trails are rerouted, regulations change, techniques evolve, facilities come under new management, etc.

We appreciate hearing from you concerning your experiences with this guide and how you feel it could be improved and kept up to date. While we may not be able to respond to all comments and suggestions, we'll take them to heart and we'll also make certain to share them with the author. Please send your comments and suggestions to the following address:

Globe Pequot
Reader Response/Editorial Department
246 Goose Lane, Suite 200
Guilford, CT 06437

Thanks for your input!

Paddling Alaska

Kayak, Canoe, Paddleboard, and
Raft the Greatest Fresh Waters in the State

Second Edition

Dan Maclean

FALCONGUIDES

ESSEX, CONNECTICUT

An imprint of Globe Pequot, the trade division of The Rowman & Littlefield
Publishing Group, Inc.
4501 Forbes Blvd., Ste. 200
Lanham, MD 20706
www.rowman.com

Falcon and FalconGuides are registered trademarks and Make Adventure Your Story is a trade-
mark of The Rowman & Littlefield Publishing Group, Inc.

Distributed by NATIONAL BOOK NETWORK

Photos by Dan Maclean unless otherwise noted
Maps by Melissa Baker and The Rowman & Littlefield Publishing Group, Inc.

British Library Cataloguing in Publication Information available

Library of Congress Cataloging-in-Publication Data
Names: Maclean, Dan, author.
Title: Paddling Alaska : kayak, canoe, paddleboard, and raft the greatest fresh waters in the state /
    Dan Maclean.
Description: Second edition. | Essex, Connecticut : Globe Pequot, [2023] | Series: Paddling series
    | Includes index. | Summary: "Paddling Alaska describes the best and most accessible routes—
    forty classics in all, from downtown Anchorage to the Matanuska and Susitna Valleys and the
    Kenai Peninsula, and from the southern interior north to the Yukon"—Provided by publisher.
Identifiers: LCCN 2022050030 (print) | LCCN 2022050031 (ebook) | ISBN 9781493067343
    (trade paperback) | ISBN 9781493067350 (epub)
Subjects: LCSH: Canoes and canoeing—Alaska—Guidebooks. | Kayaking—Alaska—Guidebooks.
    | Alaska—Guidebooks.
Classification: LCC GV776.A4 M33 2023   (print) | LCC GV776.A4   (ebook) | DDC
    797.12209798—dc23/eng/20221116
LC record available at https://lccn.loc.gov/2022050030
LC ebook record available at https://lccn.loc.gov/2022050031

A book on river voyages may really deal with the whole country
so far as the summer is concerned.

—*Hudson Stuck*, Voyages on the Yukon and Its Tributaries

Contents

IV. Northern Interior

V. Southern Interior

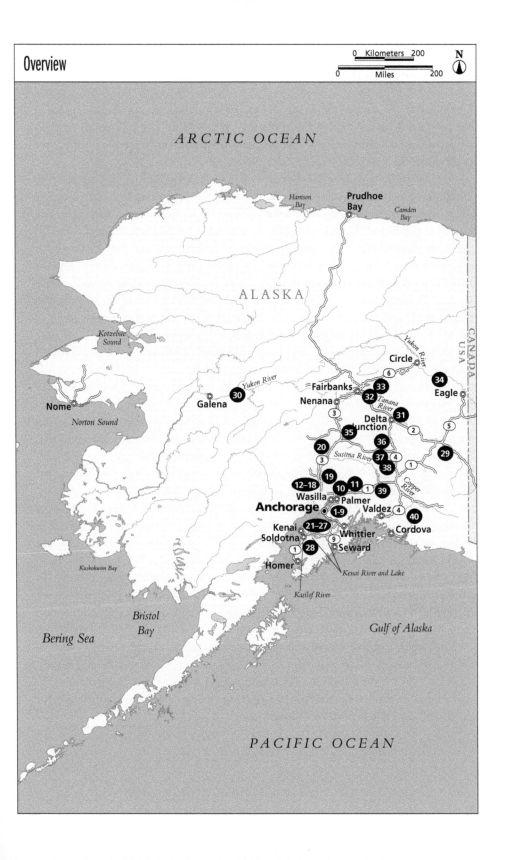

0   Kilometers   200

0   Miles   200

N

ARCTIC OCEAN

Harrison Bay

Prudhoe Bay

Camden Bay

ALASKA

CANADA
USA

Kotzebue Sound

Yukon River

Circle

⑥

Yukon River

③④ Eagle

Nome

Norton Sound

Galena

③⓪

Yukon River

Fairbanks

Nenana

③③

③②

Tanana River

③①

②

⑤

③⑤

Delta Junction

③

③⑥

③⑦ ④

③⑧

②⓪

Susitna River

③

①⑨

①②–①⑧

Wasilla

①⓪ ①①

Anchorage

Palmer

①–⑨

③⑨

①

Copper River

②⑨

Valdez

④

④⓪

Cordova

②①–②⑦

Kenai

Soldotna

⑨

Whittier

① ②⑧

Seward

Homer

Kenai River and Lake

Kasilof River

Kuskokwim Bay

Bristol Bay

Bering Sea

Gulf of Alaska

PACIFIC OCEAN

Acknowledgments

This book is the result of more than two decades paddling around Alaska. Any list of the personal debts accumulated over those years would fill this guide from cover to cover, leaving no room for maps or paddling directions. But there have been some people over the years that must be acknowledged.

My group of friends in Anchorage make Alaska's largest city a great place to live. Jessica Cochran and Nathan Pannkuk have done everything from watching my water-fearing dog to putting me on the radio and believing in my stories when few other people would. Kirsten and John Hoppe have been constant, helpful friends since the Missoula days. Jac Summers has read manuscripts and babysat Bronwyn while I wrote. Justin Bachor retrieved my paddle after a capsize. Diana DeFazio, Brooks and Rita Wade, and Kristiann Rutzler did manuscript reading under deadline. Colleen Shannon made my previous book *Paddling the Yukon River and its Tributaries* both possible and handsome with her unusual artistic skill, as well as hard work.

My old DC buddies are still my personal base. There are few pleasures more profound than constant friends through the many phases of life. Richard Craig and Tom Lalley flew up from down south to float rivers, as well.

Brooks and Rita Wade have done more than any non–family members to make this project possible. From lending me their canoe for a trip down the Little Susitna River, to fielding calls from the Alaska State Police the following morning asking for a description of that canoe, they have been patient, enthusiastic, and wonderful friends throughout the years. Brooks and his raft retrieved my beloved canoe from a flood-stage Gulkana River. And the Copper River, as well as the Kenai, Nelchina, and Tazlina, were sublime floats through wonderful country with great people.

Of course, as I have been reminded, and now understand better since becoming a parent myself, you can never thank your parents enough. My father, John N. Maclean, taught me to paddle and instilled a lifelong love of water. He took me on my first multi-day canoe trip down the Potomac River from Harpers Ferry to Great Falls. He survived—with a relieved smile and stories that are funny only in retrospect—an attempted portage down the aptly named Haggard Creek Trail. My mother, Frances, and my father have graciously encouraged my best instincts over the years, even when those instincts were not always clear.

The major debt in this book, however, is to my wife, Kristiann, and our children. From driving me for days to put-ins in the Brooks Range, to honeymooning on the Swanson River Canoe Trails, to shouldering the burden of constant rescheduling, absences, and writing time, Kristiann has made this book, and all else constructive and worthwhile in my life, possible. Thanks.

Introduction

Any book brave enough to have the title *Paddling Alaska* implies at least a degree of complete coverage of the state. However, Alaska has tens of thousands of miles of rivers, not including lake shorelines. The state is one-third the size of the Lower 48 combined. Any guide to paddling this water, by necessity, must tighten its focus.

You can also drive to all the lakes and rivers described in this guide. This fact might sound unremarkable, but Alaska is mostly wilderness, with few highways. This is the first statewide guidebook to organize journeys in this manner.

Furthermore, these floats have been carefully chosen to largely be within the ability of the average paddler. The water in this book is overwhelmingly Class I and II, and, by definition, within the technical ability of most beginner to intermediate paddlers. The trips are concentrated within easy driving distance of the population centers of this enormous state, providing quick access to wilderness for city residents and visitors alike. Some of these trips are even within city boundaries. A few are quite remote and rarely paddled. The majority of these trips, however, are considered classics, even though a few are appearing in a guidebook for the first time.

A GPS receiver is an invaluable aid in finding your way in and out of the woods. With that in mind, I've provided GPS coordinates, when available, for many of the trailheads using UTM (Universal Transverse Mercator coordinate system).

Alaska has few roads, but even fewer trails—only a few hundred miles of maintained footpaths outside cities exist. Paddling is the best way to get off the beaten track and explore Alaska's wilderness: the thousands of miles of rivers and lakes are nature's trails.

Paddling is also a comfortable, practical form of travel through this country. In a boat, it is possible to carry large loads of food and warm clothing. Open rivers and lakes are windswept, keeping the notorious, swarming Alaska bug population bearable most of the time. Gravel bars and lakeshores make ideal camps: well drained, open, and available to the public, almost always without a permit. Bears are much less likely to wander onto a gravel bar than onto a shore-based camp. River currents allow quick travel, sometimes as much as 70 miles a day on swift water.

Enjoy floating these waters. Drifting along, letting the current do most of the work, there is no finer way to see the great state of Alaska.

Paddling Alaska's Freshwater

Although the basic motions of paddling a boat are the same in Alaska as anyplace else in the world with water, there are many modifications and special situations that are only encountered in this far northern state. This section discusses them in detail.

Water Class and Hazards

Get any group of Alaska paddlers together, and, at some point, the conversation will drift onto the topic of water classification. Claiming special status for cold water and remoteness, some people argue that the International Class Rating System should be modified for Alaska by adding one point to the normal rating.

This book does not do that because it defeats the purpose of having a rating system: a clear, repeatable description of the water type encountered. Therefore, the International Class Rating System is strictly followed within these pages: Class I, flatwater; Class II, riffles; and Class III, waves and obstacles capable of swamping a boat unless it is skillfully handled.

But the class rating does not adequately describe all dangerous situations. So, for each trip in this book, a description of the difficulties encountered is given. This includes the class rating, along with a further description of other, unclassified hazards, such as frequent sweepers or strong winds. The classified and unclassified hazards are weighed together and each river is described as being suitable for beginner, advanced beginner, intermediate, advanced intermediate, or expert paddlers. This system hopefully allows a more accurate description of both the water type encountered and the overall skills required to safely navigate it.

If a trip is described as suitable for beginners, that means the water is flat and a good place where a novice can learn the fundamentals of paddling: balance, steering, boat entry and exit, etc. Advanced beginners should be able to steer the boat well and are in the process of learning to read moving water. Intermediate paddlers should have very good to excellent boat control as well as water-reading ability, and be especially good at hazard avoidance. Advanced intermediate paddlers should be able to handle extended Class III rapids without capsizing. Advanced paddlers should be able to handle anything a river can conceivably throw at you, plus a few things you can't conceive of. All of these trips, even the beginner trips within sight of homes, require considered judgement—even a city lake can be churned into waves by weather. And almost all these trips require wilderness travel experience.

Hypothermia

Alaska water is particularly unforgiving of capsizing. The water is frigid; if you flip the boat, the chill can quickly paralyze your lungs and sap your strength. Even if you do manage to swim to shore, hypothermia can quickly set in if you cannot dry off quickly. Furthermore, river water is frequently so laden with silt that if you flip the boat, your clothes can fill with sediment, quickly dragging the strongest swimmers below the surface. There are many, many places where, if you capsize, you will probably die. It should be assumed that every body of water in this book is dangerously frigid unless it is clearly stated that the water can be swimmably warm at certain times of the year and in certain, rare, weather conditions.

Braided Streams

Braided stream channels are frequently encountered, and much more difficult to navigate than a conventional channel, but are unaddressed in the water classification system. Braided streams flow from the foot of glaciers. Braided streams flow from the foot of glaciers. Glaciers are nature's bulldozers, grinding the mountains beneath the ice into tremendous quantities of gravel, sand, and silt. All this material washes out with the melting ice, choking the channel for, sometimes, hundreds of miles from the end of the ice. Floating on this water, you will hear the constant rasping of sand grains against the hull. The water flowing through these gravel bars is usually flatwater, with the occasional riffle and chop, technically Class I to Class II.

Braided channels can be extremely difficult to navigate, even for practiced experts. The many gravel bars and islands present a perpetual problem of route choice, forcing the paddler to always think ahead and try to guess what the channel around the next bend will look like. Stringers of water can peel off the main channel, leaving just a trickle of water and a grounded boat, requiring a long drag. While walking through the water and scraping the boat over gravel, you will discover that the shallows are suddenly cut off as you take a step into hip deep, swift water. Always test the depth of the water before you commit your momentum to a step. The current can also undercut banks, leaving strong trees hanging in the water as sweepers. Swift water can take you into the hanging branches, knocking you from the boat or, in the worst case, holding you under water. This guidebook clearly discusses and maps sections of this stream type, but paddlers should always be aware that these channels are constantly changing. Any map is out of date five minutes after it is made, and travelers on this stream type should expect to do original channel reading and navigation at all times.

Sweepers

Sweepers—trees leaning across the channel, with their downward branches sweeping the surface—are another constant Alaska hazard that many outside paddlers have not often encountered. On narrow creeks, they can be an almost perpetual hazard. A few people drown every year from getting caught in these tricky branches. Spruce trees tend to make the strongest sweepers, so, if there is a channel choice, try to choose a route that will take you away from spruce-lined banks. More than any other water hazard, sweepers are much less forgiving of navigation mistakes.

Bears

More paddlers die by drowning each year than by bear attacks. It is important to keep the fear of bears in perspective. Most people seem to direct their fear of the unknown or an unfamiliar environment onto the nearest, most fearsome monster. In Alaska's

Portable electric fences around tents provide a measure of protection if bears do enter camp. However, your primary energy should be on preventing bears from coming into camp in the first place.

case, this happens to be bears, both black and grizzly. (Most Alaskans call grizzly bears "brown bears," and they are almost universally brown. Black bears are almost always black in Alaska, too. For whatever reason, the cinnamon variant of black bears common in the Lower 48 and Canada is rare here.)

Your primary energy should be put into avoiding a bear encounter in the first place. The techniques for doing this are more involved and intuitive than just buying deterrents, but they are also many times more effective.

Always choose a campsite well away from fresh bear trails. More often than not, this means camping on an open island or gravel bar, but sometimes it will require reading bluff topography and choosing a campsite where the cliffs prevent access to the shore. Although bears do occasionally swim through rivers and lakes, they are unlikely to do so regularly, which minimizes a chance encounter.

Once you arrive in camp, thoroughly walk around, paying close attention to the ground. Sometimes there are a few sets of older tracks, and that might be the most relatively bear-free spot you are likely to find within 100 miles. If there is fresh bear sign, such as recent tracks, push on to what appears to be the next decent campsite, then check again. This is much harder to do than it may seem. It can be quite discouraging to keep paddling on into the night after you thought the day was over.

Once you choose a good camp spot, do not do anything that could attract bears. Many trees on gravel bars are too weak to hang food bags from, plus black bears are easily capable of climbing trees, rendering so-called bear bags a doubtful and impractical deterrent in these circumstances. Keeping food in an airtight dry bag on the ground, well downwind of the tent works well, but using a bear-proof barrel is substantially better. Do not wash with or carry scented soaps and detergents. Do not use perfume or deodorant. Do not use citronella bug repellent since it smells sweet to a bruin's nose. It is also worth noting that portable, battery-powered electric fences are now available to string around tents at night.

Odds are, though, if you spend enough time paddling around Alaska, you will encounter at least a few bears. Most will be seen on a distant shore from the safety of a boat. Eventually, one of these bears will wander into camp. This does not have to be a problem if you act appropriately.

Stand tall and do not run. Talk in a firm, forthright voice to the bear, just like you would a bully. If circumstances permit, slapping the side of a canoe or kayak with a paddle can sound like a gunshot. Almost all bears will move on in search of an easier path. However, if given time and the above methods the bear is still not scared off, pepper spray is extremely effective. Empty the can in the bear's face. Carry at least two cans so there will be an extra if one is used. Have each member of the party carry their own can so they can help out other people in case of trouble.

Many Alaskans carry 12-gauge shotguns loaded with deer slugs or .44 Magnum pistols for bear protection. This is fine, provided you know how to handle and use a gun and understand that bears can only be legally killed without a tag in immediate defense of human life and not in defense of property.

Bugs

Bugs are atrocious from late May until the first frosts in late August or early September. While paddling, though, the breeze over the water will subdue them. But when in a sheltered camp, or when the breeze dies, mosquitoes, gnats, and/or no-see-ums can be almost nightmarish.

Paddling in early spring or late fall is a great way to avoid bugs entirely. But during the summer, measures need to be taken to prevent turning the trip into a swarming nightmare. First off, as detailed in the previous section, choose an open campsite where the wind suppresses bugs. Then, wear long-sleeved jackets and pants made of material such as nylon, heavy canvas, or assorted rain gear materials that bugs cannot bite through. A head net will be essential in some situations. Combined with these clothes strategies, bug dope will only be necessary to use on the exposed back of your hands.

Make sure your tent has no-see-um netting and seals completely. Stuff a sock into the tiny gap between where the zipper pulls meet to prevent a few mosquitoes from migrating in overnight.

Canoes versus Kayaks versus Catarafts versus Rafts

Boat type will affect the quality of your paddling trip more than any other single factor, except for maybe partners, route choice, and weather. The important thing to remember is that, although each type has relative merits, the most important factor is not necessarily the boat but, rather, the paddler: you must be comfortable and skillful with your boat. While this guide makes boat type recommendations for each trip, your experience and knowledge with the boat should be the final deciding factor. Experience is something you will have to acquire on your own, but the following discussion lays out the general advantages and disadvantages of each boat type.

Canoes can carry tremendous loads of gear, easily transporting two people and weeks' worth of food and equipment. They are easy to get in and out of, which is especially handy on rivers with lots of gravel bars when you need to hop out and drag frequently. There is also plenty of space to shift your body position around, making them comfortable boats to paddle long hours in. However, canoes require practice to efficiently and skillfully control, can be tippy, do not perform well in headwinds, and are open at the top, letting in rain and water from large waves.

Kayaks require less practice to paddle skillfully than canoes and are easy to navigate with precision since they can cut across currents—and sometimes, if you are a strong paddler, they can even go upriver. Kayaks are less affected by wind than any other paddled boat. They can even slice through large waves, provided you have a good spray skirt to prevent water from filling the boat. On the downside, kayaks are awkward to get in and out of, cannot carry very much gear by boat standards, and the paddler cannot shift positions well while sitting in the boat—something that becomes increasingly important on long trips.

Catarafts and other rubber rafts are the most stable of paddled boats, require relatively little skill to paddle, are tremendously comfortable to sit on, and can carry loads well beyond what any kayak or even the largest canoe is capable of carrying. If you are looking for a moose hunting boat or want to bring the entire family, a cataraft is what you want. They are also stable platforms to fish from. Furthermore, rafts deflate and disassemble and can be transported in a car or airplane without racks, trailers, or other special equipment. However, rafts are difficult to navigate precisely—which can be a real concern on smaller Alaska rivers that have many sweepers. They are also heavily dependent on current for propulsion and are close to impossible to handle in strong contrary winds. If you will be crossing a lake or slack current with a raft, a small outboard motor is almost a necessity. Rafts also vary widely in quality. Spend the extra money to get a top-of-the-line raft—the bulletproof material and construction will pay for itself many times over.

Boat Type Recommendations

Keeping the pros and cons of the various boats in mind, this guide makes type recommendations for each trip. In general, if the water is generally flat and not frequently subject to powerful winds, any boat type will work well.

Not only can a cataraft go through bigger water and carry a larger load than a canoe, catarafts can also carry canoes through rougher water than a canoe can float.

If there are rapids or eddies that require maneuvering and stability in rough water, catarafts and whitewater kayaks are usually recommended. In this case, all other whitewater boats will work well, including C-1 or C-2 canoes. However, to prevent the novice from seeing the word "canoe" in the recommendation and setting out into water unsuitable for open boats, those specialized canoes are not mentioned in the trip descriptions. The owners of whitewater boats are frequently experienced enough paddlers to tell from the paddling description that their craft is suitable. Following roughly the same logic, only catarafts are specifically recommended in the trip descriptions. This is to ensure that only the highest-quality rafts are used and no one sees the word "raft" and sets out in a poorly made craft inadequate for the conditions. However, even though it says "cataraft," high-quality doughnut rafts with rowing frames and self-bailing floors work perfectly well, too.

Gear

A complete recommended packing list is in appendix B of this book. There are a few crucial items, however, that can dramatically improve comfort and safety for all Alaska paddlers.

The first item is X-Tra Tuff boots. These neoprene rubber boots, usually worn by commercial fishermen, are as comfortable as a cheap pair of sneakers and prevent your feet from getting soaked in calf-deep water. Their drawback is that they must be removed before heading into rough water since boots have been known to fill with silt after capsizing, dragging the person below the water. X-Tra Tuffs are essential gear despite this remote danger because they prevent the far more likely event of hypothermia from wet feet.

As an alternative to X-Tra Tuff boots, many more-experienced paddlers wear specialized neoprene boots, which keep your feet wet but warm. These are an especially good choice for whitewater since they can be safely worn while swimming.

Another essential is, again, borrowed from the commercial fisherman's wardrobe: a waterproof two-piece rain suit of bib-overall pants and a hooded jacket. Even on the hottest days of an Alaska summer, when it rains, it gets cold. And it usually rains sideways. High-technology fabrics, ponchos, etc., just don't cut it when it's 35 degrees Fahrenheit, blowing, and pouring rain.

Which brings up sleeping bags. Only use polyester-fill bags—they stay warm when wet. My summer bag is comfort rated to −10 degrees Fahrenheit and I find that to be about right for late spring through early fall paddling.

Tents must be completely enclosed by nylon and bug screens. Make sure the tent zippers are in excellent working condition before leaving. If there is any way for bugs to get in your tent, they will find it, and you will find it difficult to sleep.

Also, bring two to three times the normal number of tent stakes. Double- and triple-staking in a star pattern helps to anchor the tent to loose sand. It also provides more surface area to pile heavy rocks on when camping on gravel bars.

An oversized plastic tarp strung completely above the tent can be very handy during rainy spells. The tarp provides shelter while erecting or rolling up the tent and/or a small porch for changing wet clothes or cooking.

A fuel-burning stove is also handy. Although outdoor fire restrictions are almost nonexistent in Alaska, there is very little usable firewood on the open gravel bars and rocky shores where paddlers should be camping to avoid bears.

Pack all gear in dry bags, except for rain gear and the tent, which will almost always be wet. They can be stored in net bags if you wish, but the rain gear should be packed in the boat in such a way that it is easy to get to in rapidly changing weather.

Drinking Water

Many Alaskan rivers are fed by glaciers and are, therefore, so silty that conventional water filters plug up in just a few strokes of the pump. Boiling the muddy water for ten minutes will kill the intestinal parasite *giardia*. Letting the boiled pot sit overnight allows time for the silt to settle to the bottom. In the morning, carefully pour the clear water into your drinking containers and discard the mud at the bottom of the pot. If you use this method of making drinking water, bring a large enough pot to boil a day's worth of water, plus abundant stove fuel.

Communication

Cell phones do not work on most of these rivers. Do not count on using one anywhere except for within the city limits of Anchorage or Fairbanks—and even within the city limits there are dead spots. On more remote waters, you will have to bring some sort of satellite communication such as inReach (with a current subscription). Rescuers will not respond to your call unless you are calling from a satellite phone with GPS coordinates. It can also be a prudent purchase to buy insurance from a medical helicopter service in advance of the trip.

The most important thing to remember is to use good judgment to minimize the chance of having to make an emergency phone call in the first place.

Walking Away from a River

If you paddle long enough, at some point water will rise unexpectedly, or some other random event will occur that makes floating too dangerous. If you are prudent and interested in paddling for a long time into the future, you will just walk away from the river. In many cases, the wisest thing to do will be to stash your boat and gear near the water and bushwhack out with a small pack. Attempting to portage is mostly useless because it lengthens the walk with gear ferrying, and the heavier loads wear you out more quickly. Leave a note on the gear explaining the situation so it does not cause someone else to panic unreasonably. Return on a friend's boat a few weeks later when the water is lower to retrieve things.

Many rivers in Alaska are too remote from roads to walk out. In these cases, just camp on high ground and wait for the water level to fall. Extra food is some of the best safety equipment there is.

The Sun

On many waters, the heat of a summer day creates wind so strong that it is difficult to paddle. But this is the Land of the Midnight Sun after all, and at night it is often light enough to see (depending on the time of year and latitude) as well as calm. It can work well to camp during the windy day and paddle through the still night. Besides being faster and safer at times, paddling through the summer night is a rare and beautiful experience. The sun can set just enough to turn the world a crimson red. Nocturnal animals wander the beaches. Paddling along at 3 a.m., you may see wolverines, wolf packs, and other animals that even longtime Alaskans have never seen. A nighttime paddle can be a fantastic experience worth doing, even if it isn't a weather necessity.

Map Legend

Transportation

=⊙= State Highway

Other Road

+—+—+ Railroad

Trails

------ Paddling/Hiking Trail

→ Direction of Travel

Water Features

Body of Water

Major River

Minor River or Creek

// Rapids

Waterfalls

Marsh

Glacier

Dyke

N
⊕ True North (Magnetic North is approximately 15.5° East)

Symbols

🚻 Restroom

卉 Picnic Area

Boat Launch

⌣ Bridge

■ Building/Point of Interest

Δ Campground

▲ Campground (primitive)

⌂ Cabin

1 Mileage Marker

P Parking

—— Trans-Alaska Pipeline

Put-in/Takeout

▲ Peak

Recreation Area

? Visitor Center/Information

Trailhead

=) (= Tunnel

I. Anchorage Area

"Anchorage is a great place to live because it is right next to Alaska," is a standard joke heard throughout the state's largest city. Just out of sight of its strip malls, wide streets, and cul-de-sacs lies easily accessible, scenic floating. Visitors from out of state will probably be shocked that such lovely and wild rivers exist so close to a large human population. They are unaware of the secret of Anchorage: that the mountains and oceans that surround the city force the urban area into a tightly confined triangle between the ocean and mountains. And Alaska begins just on the other side of those hills.

The trips chosen for this section of the book are all suitable for a quick summer's evening paddle, or an all-day float to plan the weekend around.

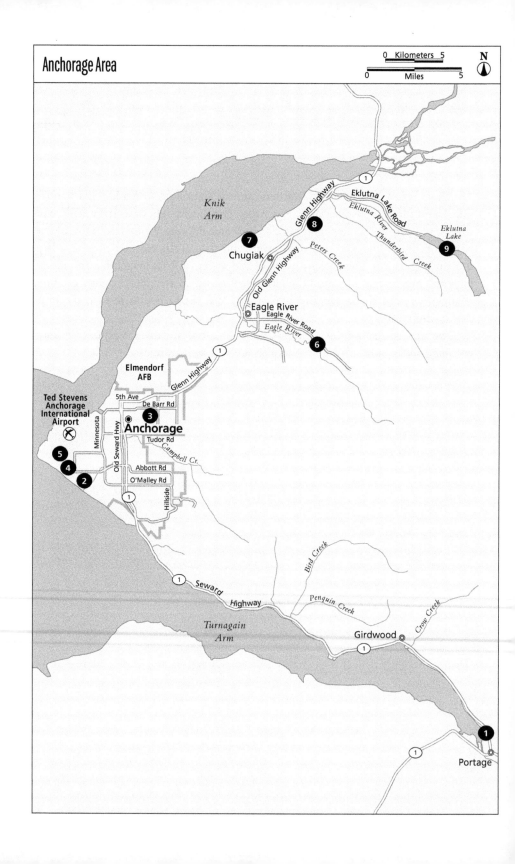

Anchorage Area

Knik
Arm

Glenn Highway

Eklutna Lake Road

Eklutna River

Thunderbird Creek

Eklutna Lake

8

7

9

Chugiak

Old Glenn Highway

Peters Creek

Eagle River

Eagle River Road

Eagle River

6

Elmendorf
AFB

Glenn Highway

1

Ted Stevens
Anchorage
International
Airport

5th Ave

De Barr Rd

Anchorage

Tudor Rd

3

Minnesota

Old Seward Hwy

Campbell Cr.

5

4

Abbott Rd

2

O'Malley Rd

Hillside

1

Bird Creek

1

Seward

Highway

Penguin Creek

Crow Creek

Turnagain
Arm

Girdwood

1

1

1

Portage

1 Portage Creek

Character: A scenic paddle down a glacier-fed creek within a short drive of Anchorage.
Distance: Between 2 and 10 river miles, depending on put-in and takeout choices.
Estimated paddling time: 1 to 5 hours.
Boat types: Flat bottom canoe, river kayak, or cataraft.
Special features: Glacial outflow and strong tides near mouth.

Difficulties: Intermediate. Class II, choppy riffles, shallow gravel bars, wandering channel, frigid water, and sweepers.
Season: Late May through the end of September.
Contact for more information: For general information, do a web search for "Begich-Boggs Visitor Center at Portage Lake, Chugach National Forest."

Overview

A scenic paddle only an hour's drive from Anchorage, a Portage Creek float reminds you that you are in Alaska, even though you are so close to its largest city. Fed by the retreating Portage Glacier, the barely melted ice and silt of Portage Creek rushes through a partially braided channel for the quick journey to the ocean. The sheer walls of the Chugach Range tower over the U-shaped valley, mountains that were underneath glaciers themselves just a few hundred years ago.

The float is a nice balance; it's both a bit of a challenge and forgiving enough for advanced beginner and intermediate paddlers to enjoy themselves. The water is frigid, so you certainly don't want to flip the boat. But the channel is narrow, and the riffles are Class II and usually clearly visible with plenty of reaction time before the boat is washed into the action. The many gravel bars are an excellent introduction to paddling braided rivers, a stream type common in Alaska but that out-of-state paddlers almost certainly will not have encountered before.

There is one strong caution that must always be kept in mind. Portage Pass separates two major climate zones: the wet, temperate weather of Prince William Sound and the drier, more continental weather of the interior. Consequently, strong air currents rushing between these two zones are funneled through Portage Valley and down Turnagain Arm. If you see whitecaps while driving along the Arm, it will probably be too windy to control the boat on most of the creek, and certainly along the mouth and lake. Just drive away that day and return sometime in the future.

General Access

There are a number of put-ins and takeouts, accommodating a number of trip lengths between 2 and 10 miles. The Seward Highway crosses the mouth of the river at the last takeout before Turnagain Arm, by the Portage Creek No. 2 bridge. It works particularly well to leave a bicycle chained to a tree in the brush before driving up the Portage Glacier Road and putting in farther upstream. This way, only a single vehicle is necessary to shuttle between the start and finish. The Trail of Blue Ice is a biking

Portage Creek

Turnagain Arm

To Anchorage

To Kenai Peninsula

Seward Hwy

Takeout
Portage Creek
No.2 MP 79.4

Placer River

Portage Creek

Portage Glacier Road

Alaska Railroad

Informal Access
Mile 2.15

Informal Access
Mile 3.4

Informal Access
Mile 5.35

Begich-Boggs
Visitor Center

Scenic
Viewpoint
Access
Mile 6.1

Portage Lake

To Whittier Tunnel

N

0   Kilometer   1

0   Mile   1

and walking trail through the forest that parallels Portage Glacier Road for most of the length. It is only necessary to bike a small part of the return trip on the road.

It is possible to put-in as far upriver as Portage Lake. As of this writing, it is illegal—and also unadvised—to paddle anywhere on the lake except in a direct line hugging the shore from the parking lot to the creek. The weather changes extremely quickly in the valley and can switch from sunny and calm to violently blowing rain within 10 or 15 minutes. *Do not paddle out into the lake.* Many times, paddlers will arrive at the lake put-in only to see large, wind-driven waves crashing onto shore. They will be well advised to put-in at the first bridge by the Begich-Boggs Visitor Center instead. They will remain within the shelter of the smaller creek channel for the beginning of the paddle.

Access Mile-by-Mile

Between Seward Highway MP79 and 78, 47.6 miles from Anchorage: Portage Creek No. 2 parking area. Park the pick-up vehicle (or bicycle) at this small lot on the southwest side of the bridge. Drive a further 0.5 miles and make a left onto Portage Glacier Road. Set the mile counter on your vehicle odometer to 0. The mile counts after this point begin at this junction.

Portage Glacier Road, mile 2.15: An unmarked, informal gravel road leads through the alders to a gravel beach beside Portage Creek. Park and put-in here if you are just looking for a quick, half-hour paddle. It is a common spot for fishermen to launch motorboats from trailers.

Portage Glacier Road, mile 3.4: Another informal gravel road heads directly to the bank and a small space for parking. It is approximately a 1-hour paddle down the creek from here to the Portage Creek No. 2 bridge.

Portage Glacier Road, mile 5.35: An unmarked gravel road leads off to the right just before the bridge guardrail, leading down to the water's edge at the lake outlet. This is an excellent sheltered put-in when the wind is blowing strongly enough to create waves on the lake. It is about a 3-hour float from here to the Portage Creek No. 2 bridge.

Portage Glacier Road, mile 6.1: Park at the scenic overlook lot to have a short paddle across the lake. *Only start from here when the weather is calm.*

The Paddling

Portage Glacier Road, mile 6.1 put-in. A gravel footpath begins on the tunnel side of the guardrail and travels 100 yards through the alders to the lakeshore. Paddle within 100 yards of the north shore on a direct route to the lake outlet.

This low water view of Portage Creek shows the channel running along the bluffs on the right bank. It is also an illustration of how much water levels can fluctuate, affecting paddling conditions. This picture was taken at the end of October when water levels are much too low to float the creek.

Portage Glacier Road, mile 5.35 put-in: Pass underneath the bridge to enter the creek. The wind can be strong here, and ice chunks can accumulate at the outlet.

Below Portage Glacier Road, mile 2.15 put-in: The creek is strongly influenced by the tide below here: Turnagain Arm has the second highest tides in North America and the water surges up the creek. Be sure to pull your boat high up the bank and securely tie it to something permanent when beaching. Double check the boat frequently, since you will almost certainly underestimate the height of the tide.

Approaching the takeout: Stick to the left bank just before the railroad and highway bridges, and hug the bank tightly as you float underneath them. The takeout is immediately after the highway bridge. The bank is steep enough that your boat cannot be seen from the road. However, you will probably want to have one person stay with the boat while the other retrieves the vehicle.

2 Campbell Creek

Character: A fun creek paddle across Alaska's largest city.

Distance: Between 2 and 10 river miles, depending on put-in and takeout choices.

Estimated paddling time: Paddling time on this narrow channel with tight bends is heavily dependent on paddling skill—the better your boathandling ability, the faster the paddle. Boat type also makes an enormous difference. The following times are for a short kayak well paddled. Double them for a canoe, or multiply by 2.5 for a raft. Include more time for inexperience. Campbell Creek Park to the Peanut Farm and Arctic Roadrunner restaurants: 0.5 hours.

Peanut Farm and Arctic Roadrunner restaurants to Taku Lake: 1.5 hours. Taku Lake to Dimond Boulevard: 1 hour.

Boat types: Short kayak or small raft.

Special features: Snags, sweepers, bridges, and creek-side restaurants!

Difficulties: Intermediate. Short sections of Class II water, sweepers, snags, deadfall blocking channel, bridges, rocks, moose, and many fishermen can be standing in the water.

Season: Late May through early October.

Contact for more information: For general information, do a web search for "Anchorage Parks and Recreation Campbell Creek."

Overview

Campbell Creek flows right through the heart of Anchorage and provides an excellent paddling fix for the paddler who doesn't want to drive out of town. This narrow ribbon of water flows the long way across the triangle of metropolitan Anchorage. You can start at Campbell Creek Park and stop at a choice of two creek-side restaurants for a burger, after the Seward Highway underpass, before continuing on.

Campbell Creek is sometimes thought of as trashy, urban water. But the diligent efforts of volunteers and the nonprofit Anchorage Waterways Council have done a tremendous amount of good, and the creek is much cleaner than its reputation. The odd bicycle or shopping cart stuck in the bank is usually whisked away fairly quickly, especially if you take some responsibility and clean up some trash yourself.

The creek is surprisingly wild: I have had to drag my boat through the trees and brush to avoid paddling around a bend with a defensive cow moose and calves blocking travel. Fishing for silver salmon and stocked trout can be good, too. Furthermore, the fast water, tight turns, sweepers, and snags make for a challenging paddle, requiring careful boat placement. A short kayak really, really helps if you don't want to get too wet. Many kids float/swim the creek in small rafts on warm days, get thoroughly soaked, and have a great time doing it.

A few years ago, some canoers started paddling down Campbell Creek before deciding it was more challenging water than their abilities were able to negotiate. They called in a helicopter to rescue them. They survived, only to become the butt of sneering comments at Anchorage barbecues long afterward. Retelling the event is not meant to discourage, but you should keep in mind that the creek is not to be taken lightly.

Campbell Creek may travel across Alaska's largest city, but it is still Alaska after all. This cow moose and her calves (well camouflaged, but subtly visible in this view) forced me to leave the channel and bushwhack with a boat to get around them.

Campbell Creek

0 Kilometer 1

0 Mile 1

N

Tudor Road

Access ➤ — Folker Street

CAMPBELL CREEK PARK

International Airport Road

Dowling Road

Minnesota Drive

Alaska Railroad

Taku Lake

TAKU/ CAMPBELL PARK

C Street

King Street

Access/ Takeout

76th Avenue

Lake Otis Parkway

Campbell Creek

Dimond Boulevard

Stormy Place

Arlene Street

Old Seward Highway

Seward Highway

Takeout

Campbell Lake

The takeout near Taku/Campbell Park is a little confusing. There are a number of parking lots at the park. When you park the pickup vehicle, walk down to the bank and make sure you can recognize the spot when floating down the river. Walk the path up to the railroad bridge and familiarize yourself with what the creek looks like.

While floating down the river, after you pass underneath the railroad bridge, stay alert for the pullover spot.

General Access

Campbell Creek is an urban stream and there are many informal, often privately owned, put-ins and takeouts. The following locations are public places: Folker Street turns south from Tudor Road. The parking spaces here are great for a drop-off but aren't the best place to leave a vehicle unattended for long periods of time. Campbell Creek Park is directly off Lake Otis Parkway, on the southeast side of the parkway's intersection with Tudor Road. The Peanut Farm and Arctic Roadrunner restaurants are on both sides of the Old Seward Highway just south of the International Airport Road intersection. Taku/Campbell Park is off of King Street when turning north off Dimond Boulevard, and off 76th Avenue if turning west from the Old Seward Highway. Campbell Creek Greenbelt access is unmarked from the road but is on the west end of the Campbell Creek bridge on Dimond Boulevard just before Arlene Street.

The Paddling

From the put-in at Campbell Creek Park at Lake Otis Parkway: the creek is fast, narrow, and fun. After passing under the Lake Otis Parkway bridge, there is a run of choppy water and straight channel before slowing and bending before the Seward Highway bridges. The Peanut Farm is on the right just before the Old Seward Highway bridge, and Arctic Roadrunner is after the bridge. Arctic Roadrunner has an easier beach to land on but is closed on Sunday. Stop and get a burger.

Campbell Creek continues on in the same character after the restaurants, with many tight bends and sweepers (although as the season progresses, the density of sweepers tends to decrease as paddlers cut them down). The Campbell Creek Greenbelt officially begins here, and although there are a few houses near the bank, there are many more trees.

When you spot the Dowling Road bridge, expect the water to be a little tricky and demand precise boat placement through the rocks.

Below the Dowling Road bridge, expect to see many people fishing the holes. When silver salmon are running in August, the fishing can be excellent.

3 Goose Lake

Character: A small lake with a beach, playground, and small waterfront restaurant.
Lake size: Roughly 6 acres.
Boat types: Any, including paddleboards.
Special features: Lifeguard on duty on sunny summer days.

Difficulties: Beginner. Class I, wind is not a problem.
Season: Late May through October.
Contact for more information: For general information, do a web search for "Anchorage Parks and Recreation Goose Lake."

Overview and Paddling

The beach on this small lake can get quite crowded on the hottest summer days. However, it is a surprisingly nice place to paddle and gets quite a lot of boat traffic. There are loons and other nesting birds on the south shore. It is a short carry from the parking lot to the beach with your kayak, canoe, or raft. Just don't paddle within the marked swimming area on the north beach and nesting area on the south beach.

Goose Lake Beach is hopping on warm summer days.

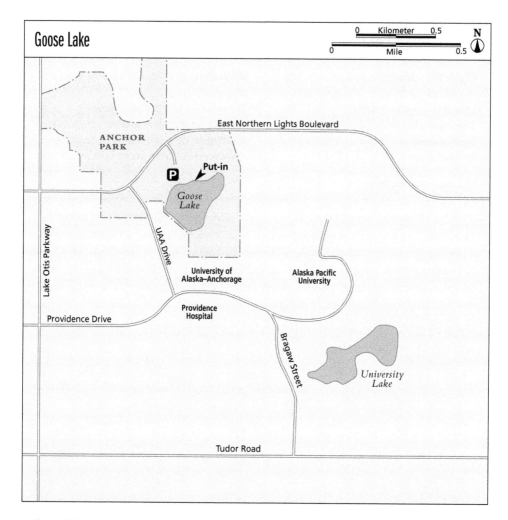

Goose Lake

Kilometer 0.5

0 Mile 0.5

N

East Northern Lights Boulevard

ANCHOR PARK

Put-in

Goose Lake

University of Alaska–Anchorage

Alaska Pacific University

Lake Otis Parkway

UAA Drive

Providence Drive

Providence Hospital

Bragaw Street

University Lake

Tudor Road

General Access

Turn at the Goose Lake Park sign on UAA Drive just south of the intersection with Northern Lights Boulevard. This is a busy intersection, and the turn is much easier to make if you are heading north on UAA Drive.

4 | Jewel Lake

Character: A small lake in an urban setting with a beach, playground, and picnic area.
Lake size: Roughly 10 acres.
Boat types: Any, including paddleboards.
Special features: Easy urban access, and lifeguard on duty on warm summer days.
Difficulties: Beginner. Class I, wind is not a problem.

Season: Late May through October.
Contact for more information: For general information, do a web search for "Anchorage Parks and Recreation Jewel Lake." To see the stocking schedule, do a web search for "Alaska Fish and Game Stocking Schedule."

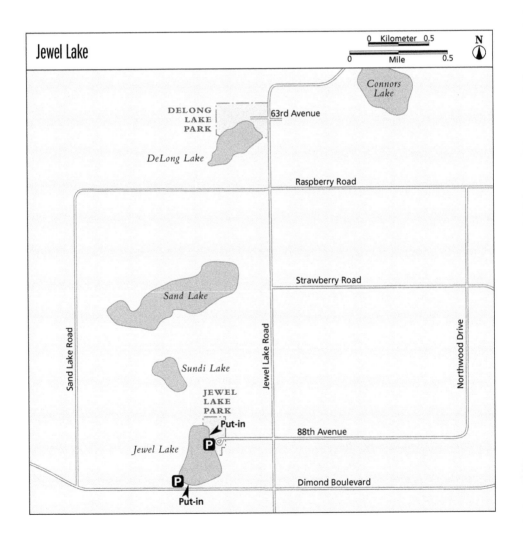

Overview

Jewel Lake has two vehicle accesses. The 88th Avenue entrance has a public beach, playground, and covered picnic area. It is a short carry from the parking lot to the water. If you are just paddling, it is a shorter, steeper carry from the parking lot to the water from the Dimond Boulevard parking area. The lake is fairly small, with many houses lining the shore. The lake is frequently restocked with fish.

General Access

From Jewel Lake Road, turn west onto 88th Avenue at the traffic light. A few blocks later, 88th Avenue ends at Jewel Lake Park.

From Dimond Boulevard, between Jewel Lake Road and Sand Lake Road, turn directly into the Jewel Lake parking lot. There is no street sign marking the turnoff, but the lake is plainly visible from the road.

5 DeLong Lake

Character: A small lake in an urban setting with a beach and fishing dock.
Lake size: Roughly 10 acres.
Boat types: Any, including paddleboards.
Special features: Easy urban access, easy fishing.
Difficulties: Beginner. Class I, wind is not a problem.

Season: Late May through October.
Contact for more information: For general information, do a web search for "Anchorage Parks and Recreation Jewel Lake." To see the stocking schedule, do a web search for "Alaska Fish and Game Stocking Schedule."

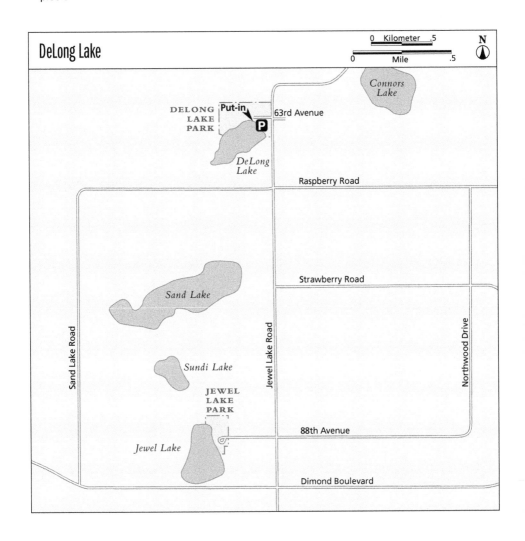

DeLong Lake

0 Kilometer .5

0 Mile .5

N

DELONG LAKE PARK — Put-in

63rd Avenue

Connors Lake

DeLong Lake

Raspberry Road

Strawberry Road

Sand Lake

Sand Lake Road

Sundi Lake

Jewel Lake Road

JEWEL LAKE PARK

Northwood Drive

88th Avenue

Jewel Lake

Dimond Boulevard

Overview

The southern shore has many houses built close to the water. However, the north shore is wooded park land. There is a fishing dock on the north shore as well. DeLong Lake seems to have the best fishing of the urban lakes mentioned here, and paddling is usually an effective way to pursue those fish. It is a great place to introduce small kids to fishing from boats because of the high fish populations.

General Access

From Jewel Lake Road, just north of the Raspberry Road intersection, turn west into DeLong Lake Park—there is a sign—almost parallel with 63rd Avenue. It is a short carry from the parking lot to the water.

6 Eagle River–Including the North Fork

Character: A scenic paddle down a glacier-fed creek within a short drive of Anchorage. There are rapids on the lower section.

Distance: 11.4 miles from the North Fork put-in to the Eagle River Loop Bridge (also called Briggs Bridge), and a further 3.3 miles to the upper campground above the Class IV Campground Rapids.

Estimated paddling time: North Fork put-in to the Eagle River Loop Bridge takeout will take roughly 2.5 to 3 hours in a kayak, and up to 4 or 5 hours in a raft. It is a further half hour from the bridge to the Eagle River Campground. Double that time for a cataraft. Paddling time is highly dependent on water level, which changes drastically over the season because the Eagle

River is fed by glaciers. The above times are based on a 2-foot water level at the Eagle River Loop Bridge marks.

Boat types: Plastic river kayak or cataraft; canoes are discouraged, especially at higher water levels.

Special features: Glacial outflow, rapids, easy access, and scenic float close to population centers.

Difficulties: Intermediate. Class I to III, sweepers, snags, frigid water, silt, pull-out above Class IV rapids.

Season: Late May through early October.

Contact for more information: For general information do a web search for "Alaska State Parks, Chugach State Park Eagle River."

Overview

Set in a deep, glacially scoured valley, the Eagle River is a wonderfully scenic rush of water that passes by a small community outside Anchorage.

The fast but relatively smooth channel of the North Fork above the bridge makes a fantastic float to plan a day around. The Class I to II water is pleasantly navigable by kayaks and catarafts, keeping a paranoid eye out for sweepers the whole flow. Wildlife viewing can be excellent. Sometimes, it can be too good: a brown bear feeding on a moose carcass on the bank shut down floating on the river one spring a few years back. It is surprising how close the wilderness gets to Alaska's most populated areas.

(As a side note, although the North Fork begins well above the mile 7.4 put-in on Eagle River Road, this guide does not recommend the general public paddle above that put-in. There is an informal parking area just above the mile 7.4 put-in, and some people park there to avoid paying the state park fee. Please don't start there. There are so many sweepers, snags, and channels dead-ending in snag mounds it should only be left to cautious experts. Having said that, pack rafting from the Crow Pass Trail crossing down to the Eagle River Nature Center is a classic run.)

The section below the Eagle River Loop Bridge (confusingly, also called the Briggs Bridge depending on the source of information) is full of rocky Class II and III rapids, with a portage path takeout just above the Class IV Campground Rapids at the end of the run. This lower section is frequently floated after work by paddlers who crave some whitewater fun at the end of the day. Many canoes are lost on this section every year, so plastic river kayaks and high-quality rafts are the only recommended boats on this section. Including the drive from Anchorage and shuttling of vehicles, the entire bridge to campground run can be done in under two and a half hours.

Below the campground, Eagle River is Class III and IV rapids. And that rough water flows through Joint Base Elmendorf Richardson, a major military base. The paperwork requirements for entry are rigid, bureaucratic, and constantly changing. Therefore, this section is not included in this guide.

I know more people who have unintentionally gone swimming in Eagle River than in any other body of water in Alaska. The water is so cold it can take your breath away and petrify your muscles. There are numerous snags and sweepers above the Eagle River Loop Bridge and lots of rocks below it. This water requires concentration and boat control throughout the paddle. Although it flows by many homes, Eagle River is not tame.

General Access

Mile 7.4 put-in: Drive 7.4 miles up Eagle River Road after dropping off the pickup vehicle downstream. It is a short carry to the bank at this parking lot operated by Alaska State Parks. There is a fee to park.

Eagle River Loop Bridge (Briggs Bridge) put-in: There is no sign marking this put-in, but turn into the right turn lane just before the bridge while heading north on Eagle River Loop Road. The parking area is operated by Alaska State Parks and the launching beach is smooth and placid.

Eagle River Campground: At Glenn Highway mile 11.6, take the Hiland Drive, Eagle River Loop exit and follow the landfill and campground signs. From Eagle River Loop Road, follow the correctional center and campground signs, paralleling the highway, taking the road down to its end at Eagle River Campground. Operated by Alaska State Parks, the paved roads of this well-used campground have ample day use parking. However, the riverside parking is after the Campground Rapids, which all but the most experienced river runners should take the portage trail to avoid. That trail enters the campground by campsite 7, and you will have to walk through the campground to get your vehicle.

The Paddling

From the mile 7.4 North Fork put-in: Walk your boat from the parking lot down the short path to the informal beach. This water can be relatively fast with tight bends. There are many, many sweepers along the banks. As you round a blind corner, sticking to the inside of the bend gives you more time to scout the river ahead and avoid more sweepers since the trees tend to fall on the outside cutbank. The profusion of turns makes plentiful gravel bars that are nice places to stop and picnic if the breeze is strong enough to keep the bugs down.

Eagle River—Including the North Fork

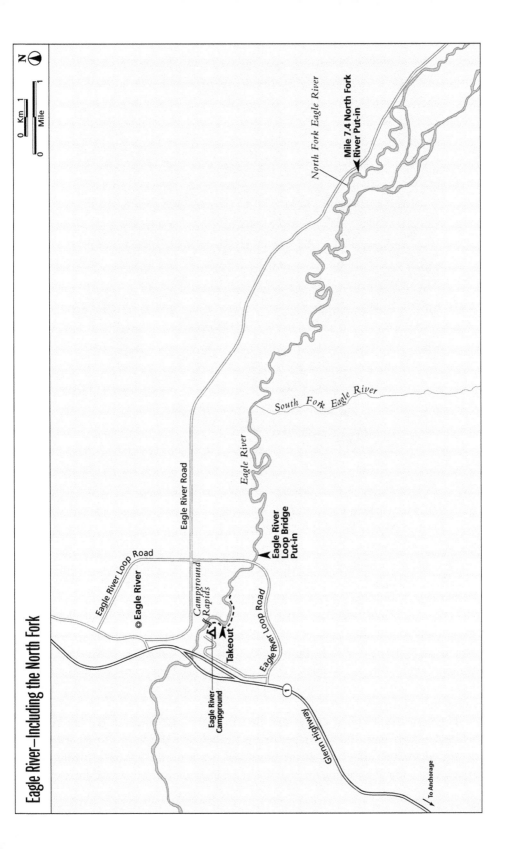

N

0 Km 1
0 Mile 1

North Fork Eagle River

Mile 7.4 North Fork
River Put-in

South Fork Eagle River

Eagle River

Eagle River Road

Eagle River Loop Road

© Eagle River

Eagle River Loop Bridge
Put-in

Campground
Rapids

Eagle River Campground

Takeout

Eagle River Loop Road

Glenn Highway

1

To Anchorage

There are few better ways to cool off on a sunny warm evening than a quick run from the bridge to the Eagle River Campground.

The channel is beginning to shift away from the road, and there are reports of catarafts struggling to find enough water to float for miles below the mile 7.4 put-in.

The mouth of the South Fork of Eagle River can be a good place to stop and fish. The clear water of this tributary makes it one of the best holes on the river.

After the contribution of the South Fork, the Eagle River begins traveling beneath high silt bluffs. There tend to be short, rocky, Class II rapids along these bluffs, which, combined with snags and sweepers in the channel, demand concentration and precise boat control. You will probably hear lawn mowers and other activity from the subdivisions built above the bluffs.

The sign danger rapids, canoes pull over in 200 yards appears at the last bend before the Eagle River Loop Bridge (Briggs Bridge). The pullout feels farther from the sign than 200 yards. Land at the broad, flat beach on the left bank before the bridge. Takeout at the parking lot here if you are in a canoe or otherwise don't want to run the rapids below the bridge. (When you park your pickup vehicle here, scout the landing to make sure you can recognize it from the water.)

From the Eagle River Loop Bridge (Briggs Bridge): There is a water-level gauge painted on a northwest bridge support. It is difficult to see from shore but easy to see once you are paddling.

The rapids begin almost right away below the bridge. They tend to be of the rock garden variety with narrow, twisting, and obscure passages between the rocks. It is very likely your boat will bash into at least one of them, and plastic hulls are recommended. The universal advice not to get hung up on something with the boat across the current holds true here, too. Paddle these rapids with at least one partner in case you flip. The water is frigid. Although there are many rocks in the channel, there are many fewer sweepers and snags than on the upper river. This section passes quickly.

Pull out at the left bank when the sign warns you to pull out. Even at lower water levels, the flow will be fast enough that it can be a scramble to land here. If you can't pull over, there is a broader, flatter spot just after the sign. But PULL OVER. A several-hundred-yard footpath leads up to the Eagle River Campground, campsite 7. There are racks along the way to rest your boat without setting it on the ground.

The Campground Rapids are below the pullout. They can be scouted from the portage path. They are real Class IV and should only be run by experts in whitewater boats, traveling in groups, with throw ropes. The day use parking area is below the rapids, on the left bank, before the Glenn Highway bridge.

7 Beach Lake

Character: A placid, stocked lake in a scenic area near Anchorage and Eagle River.
Lake size: Approximately 0.2 miles by 0.2 miles.
Boat types: Any, including paddleboards.
Difficulties: Beginner. Class I, wind and cold water.

Season: Mid-May through October.
Contact for more information: For the lodge rental, do a web search for "Eagle River Chugiak Parks and Recreation." For fish stocking information, do a web search for "Alaska Fish and Game Stocking Schedule."

Overview

Beach Lake is at the end of a dead-end road in the heart of Beach Lake Park. (Confusingly, the park municipality is the combination of Chugiak and Eagle River, although both towns are technically part of the municipality of Anchorage.) The park is closed to off-road motorized traffic, and in winter, the trails are maintained by the Chugiak Dog Mushers Association. The lake itself is stocked with fish and has good ice fishing during winter. On the southwest corner of the lake is Beach Lake Lodge, a large wheelchair-accessible lodge and cabins with electricity and running water. The buildings are available for rent through Eagle River/Chugiak Parks and Recreation. There is also a boat launch. The only thing that might disturb the tranquil scene on this lake is noise from the nearby shooting range—although you are out of rifle shot in the water, you are within earshot.

General Access

Take the South Birchwood Loop / Chugiak High School exit at mile 17 on the Glenn Highway, then head west 0.8 miles. Turn left on the unnamed gravel road, following the Beach Lake Park signs. Cross the railroad tracks and take the right at the Y, continuing another mile to the lake.

The Paddling

Put in at the launch and park in the large lot by the lake. Putter around on the pleasant lake, a quick drive from the city.

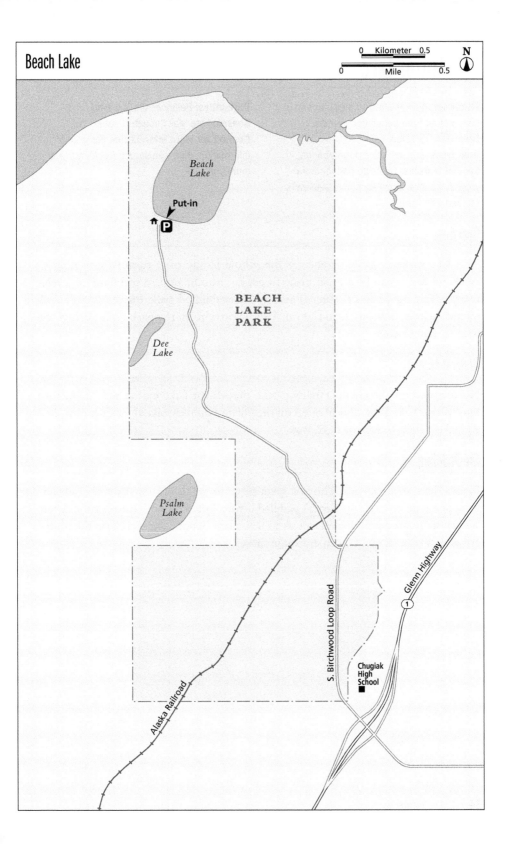

Beach Lake

8 Mirror Lake

Character: A great place to mess around in a boat, not far from population centers.
Lake size: 73 acres.
Boat types: Any, including paddleboards.
Special features: Lakeside park and playground, suitable for all ages and skill levels; stocked with fish.

Difficulties: Beginner. Class I, wind.
Season: Late May through October.
Contact for more information: For general information, do a web search for "Mirror Lake muni.org."

Overview

This lake makes a great paddle for the whole family on a summer's evening or weekend day. It can be a great place to get an introduction to paddling on a relatively forgiving body of water. There is an established park on the beach, with picnic shelters, outhouses, and so on. A short carry from the parking lot brings the boat to water's edge.

General Access

Northbound on the Glenn Highway, take the Mirror Lake exit at mile 23.6. Turn into Mirror Lake Park. Southbound on the Glenn Highway, take the exit at mile 24.5 and take a right to Mirror Lake Park.

The Paddling

Enjoy. There is no agenda. This is a great place to get accustomed to a brand-new boat, or a type of boat you haven't paddled before. Putter around. It is all good. There are private homes with float planes, as well as a Boy Scout camp beach on the southern and eastern shores. Give them some space.

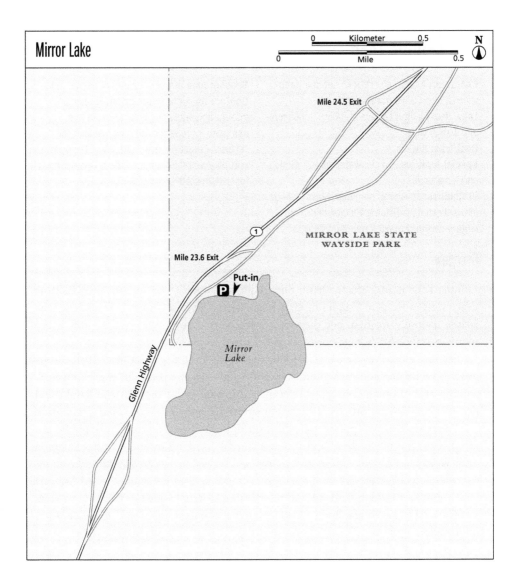

Mirror Lake

Mile 24.5 Exit

① 1

MIRROR LAKE STATE
WAYSIDE PARK

Mile 23.6 Exit

Put-in

🅿

Mirror
Lake

Glenn Highway

N

$\mathcal{9}$ Eklutna Lake

Character: A long, glacial lake set in a deep valley a short drive from Anchorage.
Lake size: Eklutna Lake is roughly 7 miles long and 1 mile wide.
Boat type: Kayaks.
Special features: Glacial water, strong winds, and long fetch.
Difficulties: Advanced beginner. Class I, wind blows down from Eklutna Glacier, churning large waves and making paddling difficult.

Season: June through the end of September.
Contact for more information: For general information, including links to cabin and campsite information, do a web search for "Eklutna Lake Chugach State Park." For boat and bike rental information, do a web search for "Lifetime Adventures Alaska."

Overview

Eklutna Lake is an L-shaped basin filled with meltwater from the retreating Eklutna Glacier. At more than 7 miles long, it is the largest lake in Chugach State Park. The lake is naturally formed, but there is a small dam at the outlet because this is the municipality of Anchorage's primary water supply.

Eklutna Lake Road ends at the lake, where there is an Alaska State Park campground, which includes two public use cabins and a day use park. The usual state-park parking and camping fees apply. Lifetime Adventures rents bicycles and kayaks and provides paddling lessons. They are headquartered in a shed near the hiking trailheads.

There are also two public use cabins on the lake itself. Yuditna Creek public use cabin is on the north shore and is also accessible on land by the Eklutna Lakeside Trail. Kokanee Cabin is on the south shore and is only accessible from the lake and is considered to be inaccessible during spring break-up and fall freeze-up. All Eklutna Lake cabins are in high demand, and reservations generally need to be made months in advance. Do a web search for "Alaska State Parks public use cabins" for reservation information.

General Access

Northbound on the Glenn Highway, take the Thunderbird Falls exit at mile 25.2. Turn right, drive past Thunderbird Falls, then turn right onto Eklutna Lake Road and drive for 10 miles until it ends at Eklutna Lake State Park. Southbound on the Glenn Highway, take the Eklutna Lake Road exit at mile 26.5. Turn east and follow the Eklutna Lake Road and Thunderbird Falls signs. Turn left onto Eklutna Lake Road and drive 10 miles to the end.

Gas motors are prohibited on Eklutna Lake. All boats must either be non-motorized or have electric motors. ATVs are allowed on the Eklutna Lakeside Trail from Sundays through Wednesdays, April 1 through November 30. The Eklutna Lakeside Trail is open to bikes and foot traffic seven days a week.

Eklutna Lake

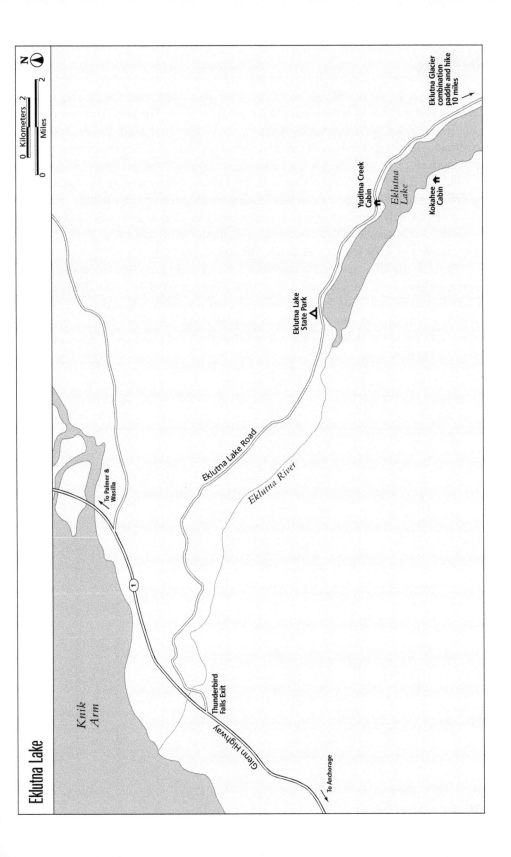

N

0 Kilometers 2

0 Miles 2

Knik Arm

To Palmer & Wasilla

Thunderbird Falls Exit

Glenn Highway

To Anchorage

Eklutna Lake Road

Eklutna River

Eklutna Lake State Park

Yuditna Creek Cabin

Eklutna Lake

Kokahee Cabin

Eklutna Glacier combination paddle and hike 10 miles

The Paddling

The put-in is informal, and you have to walk the boat down from the parking area over ground that can be quite muddy if the lake level is low. The boat rental concession leaves the kayaks at the mouth of a small creek closer to the hills and the hiking trailheads, and this ground has firmer footing but is a much longer portage from the parking area.

Eklutna Lake itself is 7 miles long, with the Eklutna Glacier feeding the upstream side. Cold wind comes ripping down off the ice, churning the water into large waves. Kayaks are the only recommended boats for this lake. Stick close to shore when paddling.

It is a 3-mile paddle to Yuditna Creek Cabin on the north shore. It is about a 3.8-mile paddle along the south shore to the Kokanee Cabin.

Traveling the full length of the lake tends to be a paddle into the wind, with a fast return paddle to the campground. But, with a following wind, it can be difficult to control the boat, and waves breaking over the stern are particularly tricky to handle. Winds are strongest in the afternoon, so keep in mind that it can become much, much windier at any time. The water is breathtakingly cold, and this is not a place you want to flip a boat.

II. Matanuska and Susitna Valleys

The Mat-Su Valley, as both the borough and wider surrounding area are popularly known, is a wide glacial outwash plain resting in a basin beneath towering mountains. As you float across the numerous rivers and lakes of this country, snow-capped peaks rise above the thick forest. The soil is fertile, and plant and animal life are abundant.

However, the Mat-Su is undergoing one of the most rapid development booms in the United States. New subdivisions, second homes, and expanded roads are exploding like mushrooms after a forest fire. On some rivers and lakes, the motorboat traffic can be so heavy that it ruins the experience for many paddlers.

The trips in this section are selected to maximize silent paddling and minimize conflicts with motorized users. On a few rivers that receive heavy motor traffic during the fishing season, this guide recommends paddling in early spring and late fall when motor use is substantially lower. After all, these are all lovely bodies of water that should be enjoyed by all.

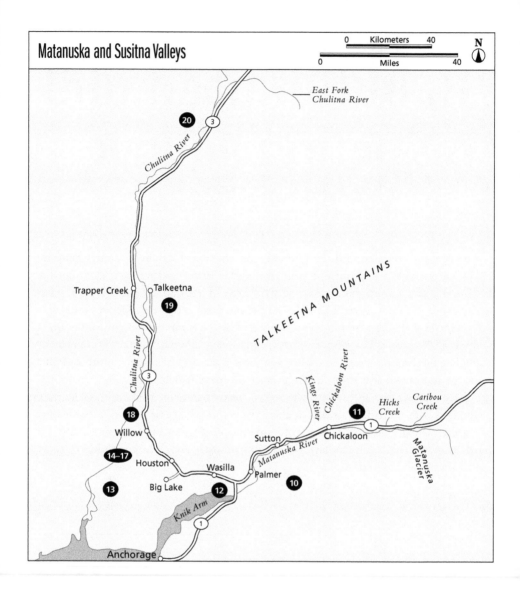

Matanuska and Susitna Valleys

0   Kilometers   40
0   Miles   40

N

East Fork
Chulitna River

⓴ ③

Chulitna River

TALKEETNA MOUNTAINS

Trapper Creek ○ ○ Talkeetna
⓳

③

Chickaloon River

Kings River

Hicks
Creek

Caribou
Creek

⓫ ③

⓲

Willow ○

Sutton ○ Chickaloon

Matanuska River

Matanuska Glacier

⑭–⓱

Houston ○

Wasilla ○

Palmer ○

⑩

⑬

Big Lake ○

⑫

Knik Arm

①

Anchorage ○

10 Knik River

Character: A wide river paddle a short distance from Anchorage, Palmer, and Wasilla.
Distance: 8 miles.
Estimated paddling time: 2 hours.
Boat types: Canoe, kayak, or cataraft.

Special features: Wide channel and strong tides near mouth.
Difficulties: Beginner. Class I, small boiling eddies and wind.
Season: Late May through October.

Overview

This wide river is a classic afternoon or evening river float. The water is Class I, so it is a good place to become accustomed to paddling on big channels. Meltwater from the Knik Glacier feeds the river, so the water is cold, but the channel below the Old Glenn Highway bridge is not heavily braided. Tides from Cook Inlet

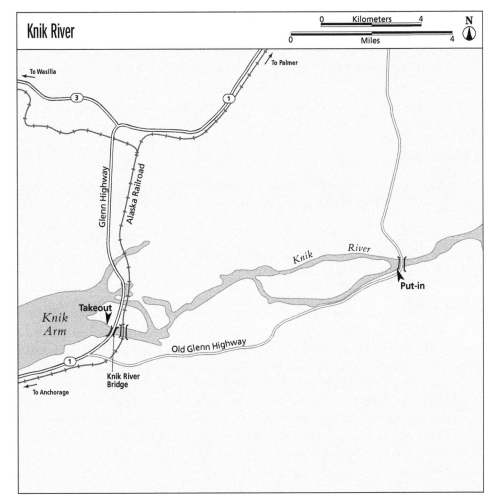

The Knik River flows beneath Pioneer Peak and the Alaska Railroad bridge.

affect the mouth of the river and may slow the paddling a bit. Consult a tide chart before leaving.

General Access

Put-in: Park at the informal gravel area on the southwestern side of the Knik River Bridge on Old Glenn Highway, near the turnoff for Knik River Road.

Takeout: Take the Knik River Access exit at mile 30.6 on the Glenn Highway. Follow the road and park by the river. It is an informal takeout area, but it is easy to launch or retrieve boats from trailers.

The Paddling

At typical water levels, there are broad, exposed sandbars throughout the river. This is a good place for advanced beginners to be coached by intermediate paddlers to learn to read channels and pick the shortest, fastest routes around bends on big rivers. Numerous islands make pleasant stops for picnics. After passing under the railroad bridge, start holding to the right shore for the takeout just after the Glenn Highway overpass. Do not miss this takeout; the next stop is Knik Arm, and you don't want to go there.

There may be the noise of four-wheelers, gunshots from the Butte, or highway noise from the Glenn Highway. The scenery is amazing, but there are many people around.

11 Matanuska River–Caribou Creek to Old Glenn Highway

Character: A fast, powerful glacier-fed river whose channel is constantly changing; world-class scenery.

Distance: Approximately 50 linear miles; the actual distance paddled will be longer due to the wide channel.

Estimated paddling time: Caribou Creek to Keith's Road (Lions Head Rapids)– 1 hour; Keith's Road to Hicks Creek–1 hour; Hicks Creek to Chickaloon River– 3 hours; Chickaloon River to Kings River– 3 hours; and Kings River to Old Glenn Highway–3 hours.

Boat types: Cataraft. Canoes and most kayak types are not recommended.

Special features: Spectacular scenery with exciting water and channel reading for experienced paddlers. There are lots of good camping spots. For a road accessible river, there is lots of wildlife and a remote feel.

Difficulties: Requires expert-level paddling skills; multiple Class IV rapids, constant original channel reading, braided river.

Season: Late May through October.

Contact for more information: NOVA River Guides the Lions Head Rapids, which is the best way to scout them. Do a web search for Alaska River Forecast Center, which has water level gauges at Glacier View on the upper river, and the Old Glenn Highway on the lower river.

Overview

The Matanuska River roughly parallels the Glenn Highway from the headwaters at Powell Glacier to Palmer. The silty water churns between towering 5,000-foot peaks. The scenery is world class. Abundant gravel bars provide opportunities for bug-reduced camping. Few people float the full river, and there is lots of wildlife.

The silt load and power of the Matanuska combine to make challenging paddling. At the head of the river, Lions Head Rapids is Class IV, with decreasing frequency of Class IV rapids as the flow continues. There are many heavily braided sections where it is a challenge to follow a channel with enough water to float the boat. The channel is constantly changing course and demands an experienced, alert paddler to navigate it.

Expert paddlers will find it a satisfying, surprisingly remote experience, all within an easy drive from Alaska's largest human population.

General Access

Warning: Always visually confirm and plan the takeout before putting your boat in the water upstream. The Matanuska channel is constantly changing, and just because a put-in or takeout is on a map—or in a guidebook—it is not necessarily there. Even if it is there, shifting currents may make the takeout difficult to impossible to reach.

Caribou Creek put-in: At mile 82, there is an easy gravel put-in at Caribou Creek. It is possible to back a trailer to the water and there is abundant parking. NOVA River Guides launches their Lions Head tours here, so be sure to leave plenty of space for them to launch and turn around.

Matanuska River

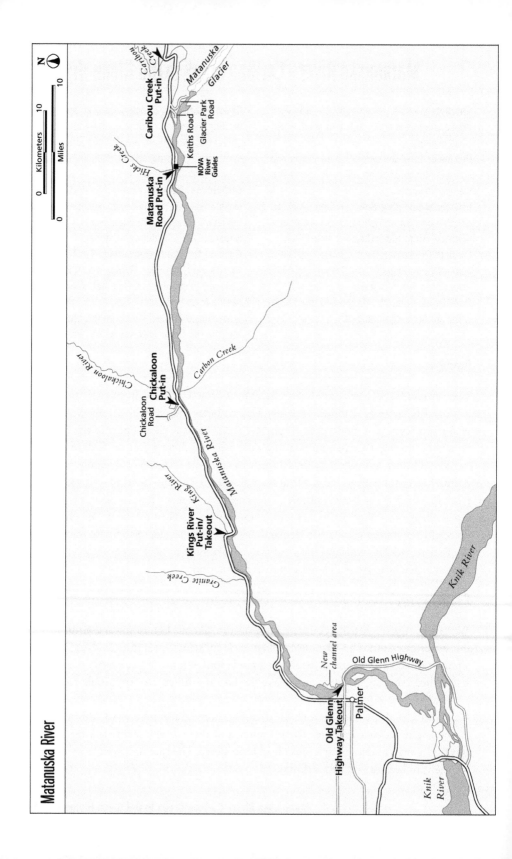

Keith's Road put-in and takeout: Keith's Road is a privately maintained gravel road. The launch area is just upstream from the bridge. NOVA river guides uses this location to launch and takeout, so please leave plenty of room for access when parking.

Hick's Creek put-in: The public access is just west of Hick's Creek on Matanuska Road. There is plenty of room to turn and park a trailer there, but the launch can be difficult. At least in some conditions, the launch is a 2-to-3-foot cutbank above flowing water, so skill and coordination are required to enter the river. It is not possible to takeout under those conditions. NOVA river guides is on the east side of Hick's Creek and the access there is private. When contacted in advance, NOVA has been known to make arrangements to launch or takeout there.

Chickaloon River put-in: When turning off the highway, the public access is almost immediately to the right off of Chickaloon Branch Road. There are no signs. The gravel road is steep and there is little room to maneuver a trailer. In some conditions, the launch is a 2-to-3-foot cutbank into flowing water, so skill and coordination are required to launch.

Almost immediately, the Chickaloon River enters the Matanuska. There are two large boulders with a large gap and potentially lethal hydraulic between them. Stick hard to the right shore to avoid the boulder gap.

Continue to stick to the right to avoid the hydraulic in the center of the river just past the Carbon Creek entrance on the left.

There is no practical way to takeout at Chickaloon.

Kings River put-in and takeout: Kings River put-in is a series of gravel bars along the King River mouth which provide informal launch and takeout opportunities. For launching, above and below the bridge can provide good access, as well as right or left of the Kings River.

Takeout here can be challenging. If planning to takeout, you must scout the takeout and its river approach in advance. Sweepers, shifting gravel bars, and so on, can all change and make a previously used takeout spot inaccessible. There is also a smaller informal gravel put-in/takeout location to the right off the Glenn Highway and just upriver from Kings River. If using this spot for takeout, eyeball the upstream currents in advance. In some river conditions, it can be very difficult to impossible to cut across currents to reach this spot in time.

Old Glenn Highway bridge takeout: The takeout is now on river right, at the Matanuska River Park bike bridge parking area. Scout this spot in advance before putting in. It is an informal takeout spot with shifting gravel bars and currents. Pull out where you can. There is a steep, bumpy four-wheel drive gravel path to the water, but there is a high likelihood of your vehicle getting stuck near the river. If needed,

Happy Hooker Towing is one of the few tow operators who does river rescues. The sure way to get from the river to the car is to hand carry the boat and gear.

Many maps and satellite photos show a takeout on river left, just downstream of the Old Glenn Highway bridge. This takeout is now closed from the road and the river channel has shifted, preventing landing there.

The Paddling

Any section of the Matanuska is now an expert-level float. Much of the upper river contains Class IV rapids. The relatively smoother water of the lower river from Kings River to the Old Glenn Highway used to be the most popular float, accessible to a broader range of padding abilities. However, for the foreseeable future, this section is dangerous and unpredictable since the shifting main channel is digging through forest and filling the water with trees.

At all times, the Matanuska is swift, cold, and silt laden. If planning to camp overnight, bring enough water from home for the whole trip, or else a large enough pot to let the silt settle from the water overnight and pour the clear(er) water off the top in the morning. The channel is always changing, and the paddler will have to read the current and make constant course adjustments well in advance of river obstacles or channel turns. Even if it has not been raining in the valley, water levels can quickly change, sometimes rising 6 inches over night from rain in the tributary hills— tie boats off well when camping. There are frequently strong upriver winds in the afternoon that can make it more challenging to control a large raft, so paddling is generally easier earlier in the morning and later in the evening.

Caribou Creek to Keith's Road (Lions Head Rapids): This a Class IV trip at normal water levels. It is routine to get knocked out of the boat on this stretch. All paddlers should wear dry suits and helmets. Travel with a minimum of two boats in sight of each other. All paddlers must be proficient in moving water rescue.

NOVA river guides leads raft trips through these rapids. It is strongly recommended that independent paddlers run the rapids first with NOVA to take advantage of the scouting opportunity.

Caribou Creek itself is a Class II tributary of the Matanuska. Its constantly changing channel provides a short warm-up before entering the Matanuska River.

Lions Head rapids are formed as the river is forced between the bluffs of Lions Head Mountain and the terminal moraine of the Matanuska Glacier at Glacier Point. As the river flows along the rocky moraine, the channel is relatively narrow, swift, and deep.

There is generally a 1- or 2-raft-sized eddy on the right just above the rapids, where boats can group up if they become separated. Lions Head rapids themselves are characterized by a repeating pattern of generally bouldery Class IV whitewater containing one or two large (4-to-6-foot drop) hydraulics per stretch of Class IV, separated by a stretch of Class III rapids before the next Class IV stretch. There are few reliable eddies or scouting locations along the rapids, so read the water while floating to choose the best route according to the current conditions. The water is swift and you will have to scramble to follow a desirable line.

The Glacier Park Road bridge is the signal to pull right and prepare to eddy out above the Keith's Road bridge if taking out there. This section is about a 1-hour float.

Keith's Road to Hicks Creek: Class IV. The water is still fast and pushy through here, and there are still sections of Class IV rapids with large hydraulics. These rapids, though, are not as large as at Lions Head, and skillful paddlers will be able to avoid the large hydraulic associated with each rapid. The intensity of the rapids decreases as the channel progresses farther from the Matanuska Glacier moraine. This section is about a 1- to 1.25-hour float.

Presently, the only takeout option is on the privately owned NOVA river guides location, just before Hicks Creek enters the Matanuska. You must call and make prior arrangements to use their beach above the high water line.

Hicks Creek to Chickaloon: Class III plus. A quick float down from Hicks Creek, the Matanuska River channel widens and develops braids. The frequent gravel bars will require constant route picking to find enough water to float the boat. When picking a route, in general, try to follow the main body of water as much as possible, while staying in the central channel to avoid the possible sweeper hazards along the far banks. If a boat does get grounded, hop out and push it off from the upstream side. If you free it from the downstream side, the current is quite swift and can suddenly catch the boat and knock you under it.

Approximately 0.5 miles above Chickaloon, the braids end and the channel consolidates into one flow. There will be larger wave trains and some avoidable rocks and turbulence along the banks through this section. A steel cable that carries a privately owned hand car crosses the Matanuska just before the Chickaloon River entrance.

There is no good takeout at Chickaloon.

Chickaloon to Kings River: Class III plus. The Chickaloon River comes in from the right. There are two large boulders with a huge hydraulic between and below them at normal water levels. It is entirely avoidable from the Matanuska by sticking to river left. Continue to stick as close to the left bank as possible as Carbon Creek enters the Matanuska on the left. The Carbon Creek delta is gravelly and braided, but at most water levels, it's possible to get the boat right next to shore as you go down. Sticking to the left avoids the large hydraulic in the center of the Matanuska just below the Carbon Creek mouth.

The Matanuska becomes more braided with the addition of Linquist Creek and Carpenter Creek on the left. There are many fine camp spots on the gravel bars through here, but eddies big enough to land a large raft are infrequent.

The channel consolidates a bit around the bluff above Kings River, but if you are taking out here, it can be a real challenge to cut across the river and currents to pull out. Always scout your takeout before putting in because sometimes the gravel bars below the Kings River mouth can be covered in water and sweepers making it impossible to land.

Kings River to Old Glenn Highway: Class III plus. This section of the Matanuska is, traditionally, the most frequently paddled. It does not have the big hydraulics and boulder rapids found on the upper river, but it is still quite challenging, especially so because of its changing channel.

Generally, the channel is mostly braided below Kings River, with rocky bluffs on the cut banks. At the end of the bluffs, large wave trains develop, along with turbulence and boils from the occasional promontory.

After Kings River, the river cuts close to the community of Sutton and the Glenn Highway. It is cutting new channel to the right through this section, as the houses hanging above the cutbank show.

Granite Creek enters directly in front of a rocky bluff, which creates a boiling back eddy on the downstream side of the delta and a downstream wave train directly in front of the bluff. It is easy to get caught in the eddy, but under most water conditions, an experienced rafter will quickly be able to get out of it.

On the approach to Palmer, there is a stretch of braided gravel bars before the main channel consolidates and turns left, downstream and away from the open gravel bars of the middle channel to the right bank. This section must be scouted in advance from the mile 50 Glenn Highway turnout. The gravel parking area is just north of the Fishhook Willow Road intersection.

The picture opposite was taken from this location. If you are able to break from the main current and follow the dashed line, it is a straightforward float through gravel bars.

However, if you go left following the main current, the new channel is actively cutting through and flooding forest. It is unpredictable and extremely dangerous. This section requires a lot of skill and a degree of luck to navigate. As of 2022, when this guidebook is being updated, the river is filled with downed trees in the channel and sweepers on the bank. The potential to get hung up on a hidden tree in the current is high. There may be log jams in the middle of a strong current, which can flip and trap a boat and paddlers. Sweepers line the bank. It is heart-in-your-mouth paddling, requiring constant, careful route picking with no mistakes. The new channel only ends just above the Old Glenn Highway bridge.

At some point in the future, the trees will wash away and leave gravel bars. What exact time that will be is impossible to predict. In the meantime, be wary of this section.

The takeout now is on the right side of the bridge. There is a prominent rock just above the bridge that forms an eddy behind it, but this is tricky to land. A more reliable spot is the gravel bars just below the bridge. Like all takeouts on this river, you should scout it in advance since it all can change quickly. The takeout used to be on the left side, but it is not possible to land on the left.

Scouting the lower section of the Matanuska River from the Glenn Highway bluffs is essential before paddling. On this smoky summer day, the mountains are hazy, but the channels are clear. The solid line shows the path of the main current, which leads behind the tree covered island and into a new channel which can be choked with fallen trees. The dashed line shows the route to take to avoid the new channel. All paddlers should scout this section from the Glenn Highway before paddling since conditions can change even from day to day.

Also notable in this view is the regrowth of woody vegetation on the right-side gravel bars. The entire channel is rising on the right side and tilting to the left, causing the creation of the new channel. Hydrology and geology in action.

12 Rabbit Slough

Trip summary: A tidal paddle with a wide variety of other recreation options.
Distance: Up to roughly 3 miles out and 3 miles back.
Estimated paddling time: Roughly 1 hour down to the lowest point easy to paddle back up from.
Boat types: Canoe or kayak.
Special features: You can paddle up and down the creek. There can be excellent fishing and bird hunting in-season. In the fall, you can paddle to ice skating on the side marshes.

Difficulties: Class I, paddling against the current and changing water levels with tides; motorboats can be common during fishing and waterfowl seasons.
Season: Late May through mid-October.
Contact for more information: For general information about the area, do a web search for "Alaska Fish and Game Palmer Hay Flats." Also, consult the fishing regulations and waterfowl seasons to determine times of peak motorboat activity—do a web search for "Alaska Fish and Game Fishing Regulations Wasilla Creek Rabbit Slough."

Overview

Rabbit Slough is a small tidal creek that takes you out and back along the Palmer Hay Flats. You can paddle up and down the creek. This route provides access to a wide range of possible resources and activities. There can be excellent silver salmon fishing in August. The marshes on either side of the banks are thick with waterfowl. And, sometimes in the fall, the marshes freeze before Rabbit Slough, so you can paddle to ice skating.

General Access

Put-in and takeout: There is an established and maintained boat launch and parking area right on Rabbit Slough. To drive there, leave the Parks Highway east of Wasilla at the Trunk Road exit, then follow Fireweed Road and Rabbit Slough Road—both of which roughly parallel the west side of the Glenn Highway— to the put-in. There is a concrete ramp into the water for boat trailers. Parking gets tight during peak salmon and waterfowl seasons.

The Paddling

You can paddle upriver or downriver from the put-in.

If heading upriver, after only one or two bends, there is a decent fishing hole. Paddling against the current above the hole quickly get challenging, so few paddlers go past there.

Heading downstream, there are sometimes large trees in the water, but it is not a problem since the current is so slow. Watch the direction the seagrasses are pointing in the water to determine which direction the tide is flowing. If the water is silty and

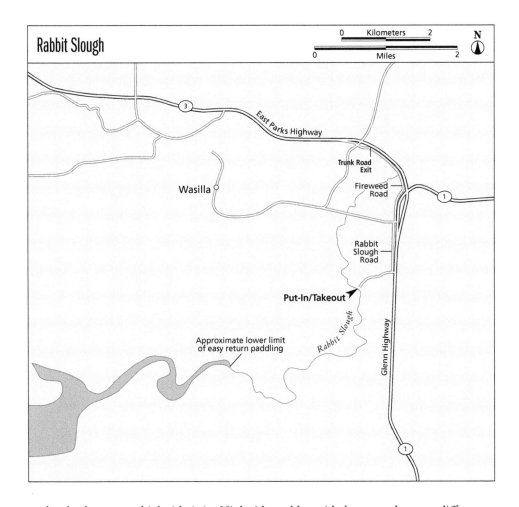

Rabbit Slough

East Parks Highway

Trunk Road Exit

Fireweed Road

Wasilla

Rabbit Slough Road

Put-In/Takeout

Approximate lower limit of easy return paddling

Rabbit Slough

Glenn Highway

cloudy, that means high tide is in. High tide and low tide here are always at different times than the published Anchorage tides, and I have never been able to figure out a formula for how they differ. For paddling, the tides don't matter a great deal since it is possible to paddle with and against the current relatively easily. For fishing, a rising tide can both push new fish into the channel as well as temporarily wipe out a hole. Tie boats off well to the bank when spending time on shore.

It is about 45 minutes to an hour of downstream paddling before reaching a point where it can be difficult to paddle back—the point is shown on the map. On the creek, this is about two major bends after leaving the trees.

You will see where the fishing holes are by the wear on the banks. Camping is also pleasant on the lower part of the paddling.

The return paddle will take only slightly longer than the paddle down if using a solo kayak or if there are two strong paddlers in a canoe.

Check Alaska Fish and Game fishing regulations for motorboat restrictions, which can change. Presently, motors greater than 3 horsepower are not allowed on weekends from July 15 to August 15— the peak of the silver salmon run. Otherwise, motorboat traffic can be thick on weekends during the tail end of salmon season and the opening of waterfowl season. When you hear the boat coming, pull along the bank to allow them plenty of room.

13 Little Susitna River

Trip summary: A great small river float across the Susitna Valley.

Distance: 39 miles. 13.5 miles from the put-in to the Nancy Lake portage trail.

Estimated paddling time: Approximately 12 hours of paddling. Allow 3 days and 2 nights for a leisurely float from the Parks Highway to Burma Landing, and 1 day to paddle from Parks Highway to the Nancy Lake portage trail.

Boat types: Canoe, kayak, or small cataraft. A boat you don't mind scraping over rocks is especially nice.

Special features: A lovely introduction to Alaska floating on a forgiving small creek. There can be lots of wildlife, such as moose, black bears, eagles, and strong salmon runs.

Difficulties: Advanced beginner. Class I to II, riffles and shallow water where you have to hop out of the boat and drag it over rocks; motorboat traffic can be especially hazardous on this narrow body of water.

Season: Late May to early June, and late September through early October.

Contact for more information: For general information about the Nancy Lake Recreation Area, do a web search for "Alaska State Parks Nancy Lake." For information about the campground and parking at the takeout, do a web search for "Little Su Campground" for the latest information about fees, reservations, parking, and so on.

Overview

Starting at Hatcher Pass, and flowing through the north edge of Wasilla, the Little Su—as it is nicknamed—does not really become floatable with a boat you want to use for a long time until the river reaches the Parks Highway. This guide begins on the downstream side of the highway.

The many tight bends of the river make for fun paddling. At most water levels, there will be shallow, rocky sections where you will have to get out and drag the boat, but most of the paddling is relatively easy in the steady current. The most hazardous thing you will encounter on this narrow channel is speeding skiffs. This guide only recommends paddling in late May or in September, when motorboat traffic is substantially reduced. When you do hear a skiff, hug the bank since many boat drivers come flying around blind corners. Few will slow down as they pass.

There are numerous camping spots on the gravelly river bends. This is a great float at the peak of the fall foliage in September. Many people do this trip annually. Roughly halfway through the trip, there is also a trail connecting the Little Susitna with the Nancy Lake Canoe Trails. Floating down the river and then portaging and paddling back up the lakes is a great trip that is uncommonly done. It also makes the vehicle shuttles much faster.

General Access

Put-in: The Parks Highway crosses the Little Susitna River at mile 57. Drive to the commercial area on the south side of the highway at mile 57.4, then follow the

Little Susitna River

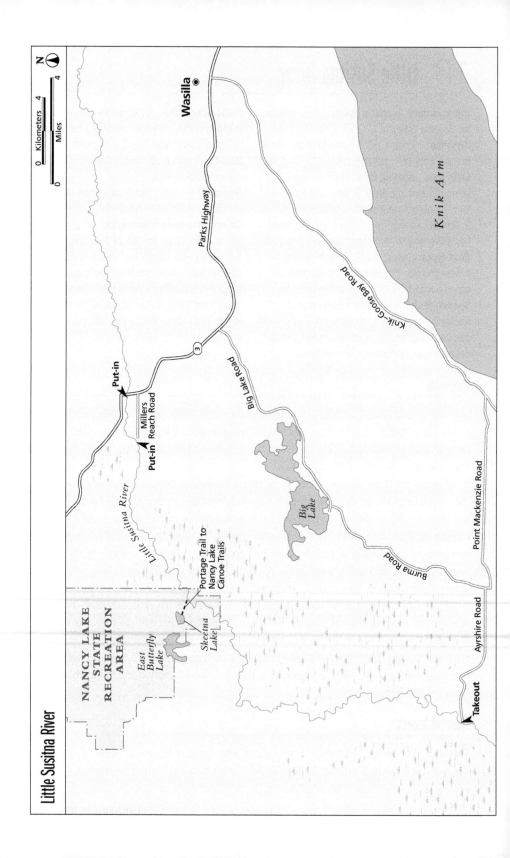

Put-in

Millers Reach Road

Put-in

Parks Highway

3

Big Lake Road

Knik–Goose Bay Road

Wasilla

Knik Arm

NANCY LAKE STATE RECREATION AREA

Little Susitna River

Portage Trail to Nancy Lake Canoe Trails

East Butterfly Lake

Skeetna Lake

Big Lake

Burma Road

Point Mackenzie Road

Ayrshire Road

Takeout

N

0 Kilometers 4

0 Miles 4

frontage road that parallels the highway to the river. It is a very short carry from the parking lot to the bank. There are no fees to park here; there is a public bathroom but no other developed facilities.

Millers Reach put-in: Turn west off the Parks Highway at mile 56.1 onto Millers Reach Road. Drive to end of the road to the reach the river. Most rafters put in here to skip slower water just below the Parks Highway.

Takeout: Little Susitna River Public Use Facility (more commonly called Burma Landing). Turn onto Point Mackenzie Road from Knik–Goose Bay Road. When Point Mackenzie Road dead-ends at a T, turn right, then follow the section line left onto Ayrshire Road. It is a 13.5-mile drive from the junction with Knik–Goose Bay Road. You can also reach Ayrshire Road by turning onto Burma Road from Big Lake Road. This is a more direct route between put-in and takeout. At Burma Landing there are fees for parking, camping, and using the boat launch ramp. The campground is operated by a private contractor of the Alaska Department of Fish and Game. Alaska State Park annual parking stickers are not valid.

The Paddling

There are many tight bends in the river down from the highway. After passing beneath the railroad bridge, there will be very few more homes on the bank. Almost every sandbar on the bends will have evidence of a camp by fall. Roughly 3.5 miles from the highway, the river passes the Millers Reach put-in.

It is a 13.5-mile paddle from the highway to the Skeetna Lake and Tanaina Loop Canoe Trails trailhead. A sign marks the trailhead, but it is subject to neglect and vandalism and may not always be standing in an obvious manner. The GPS coordinates for the trailhead are N61.59252' / W150.03543'.

There are few distinct landmarks through this forested, rolling country. A GPS receiver can help keep track of progress. It is also handy if you plan to camp and walk into the woods to moose hunt since it can be very disorienting and difficult to find your camp again.

The current slows through the sloughs when the Little Su turns more or less due south. The pace picks up again a few miles above Burma Landing. Trails worn by fishermen that begin appearing on the left bank warn of the upcoming landing. The landing and boat launch are on the left bank and easy to spot.

Nancy Lake State Recreation Area and Canoe Trails

Overview

Just 25 miles up the Parks Highway from Wasilla, in the fastest growing borough in Alaska, sits a recreational gem: the Nancy Lake Canoe Trails. This series of ponds and lakes connected by well-maintained portage trails takes the traveler across rolling, forested country that looks like northern Wisconsin and Minnesota before those states were developed. The birch and poplar trees covering the mounded hills are lovely in the fall when the leaves are turning color, and there are fewer people (and bugs) around. Hunting is not allowed within the recreation area, but the fishing action can be steady.

There are many well-maintained camping areas, as well as thirteen public use cabins that make inviting stops throughout the recreation area. The possibilities for trips are only limited by your imagination. They range from a family-friendly stay on Nancy Lake, where you can walk or paddle under a mile to one of four public use cabins, to a full loop over the Tanaina Lake Canoe Trails, taking two days or so to travel the distance of the system. Or, you can float down the Little Susitna River and follow the portage trail into the Tanaina Lake system for nearly a complete loop.

Canoe rentals can be arranged through Tippecanoe Rentals based in Willow and at South Rolly Lake. They store boats at Nancy Lake, Tanaina Loop, South Rolly Lake, and Red Shirt Lake trailheads.

As a further note, although this is a paddling guide, the lakes are wonderful to explore in the winter. Renting a cabin on Nancy Lake to use as a base camp for cross-country skiing loops is a pleasant way to spend a February weekend—a toasty fire in the stove is especially appreciated after an evening ski under the northern lights. There are also a number of marked snow machine trails.

These trips are largely free form, and it is impossible to define every possible trip within the Nancy Lake area. The format this chapter will follow is suggestions for a few longer trips from which other trips can be created.

General Access

From mile 67.3 on the Parks Highway, turn onto Nancy Lake Parkway. The parkway is paved, has clear mile markers, and is well signed. Alaska State Parks parking fees apply throughout the recreation area, and your annual Alaska State Parks parking sticker is valid here.

Nancy Lake State Recreation Area and Canoe Trails

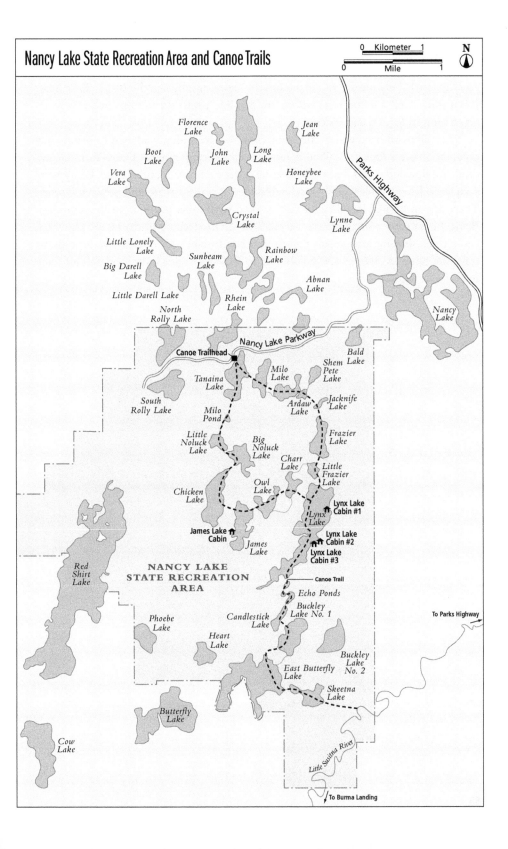

Public Use Cabins

Alaska State Parks operates and maintains the series of cabins in the Nancy Lake State Recreation Area. Online reservations are possible up to six months in advance, or seven months for Alaska residents.

The cabins all have wood-burning stoves. You are strongly advised to bring your own, stove-sized firewood. (The stoves are for heating, not cooking.) You can use dead and downed wood, but most areas near the cabin are scoured clean. Bring your own saw. Please leave enough wood behind for at least one fire, and preferably more. There are outhouses, but they are not stocked with toilet paper, so bring your own. Bring a light source since there is no electricity. The sleeping platforms are plywood, and a thick sleeping pad makes them more comfortable. All cabins have brooms, so leave the cabin as clean as you would like to find it. Do not leave food behind since this attracts animals.

14 Nancy Lake

Trip summary: A fantastic family weekend on flatwater with public use cabins.
Distance: 0.25 to 0.75 mile.
Estimated paddling time: 10 to 30 minutes from the put-in to the cabins.
Boat types: Canoes are the most common.
Special features: A short, gentle lake paddle.
Difficulties: Beginner. Class I, strong winds can create waves, but most paddling between the trailhead and cabins is within a sheltered area.
Season: Late May through early October.

Contact for more information: For cabin reservations, do a web search for "Alaska State Parks, Public Use Cabins Mat-Su." For canoe rental information, do a web search for "Tippecanoe Rental" to find their phone number (Tippecanoe does not have a website and conducts all business over the phone): you make an appointment with them to meet at a specific time at Rolly Lake campground to pick up life jackets, paddles, and the combination(s) to the locks on the canoes stored at the trailhead.

Overview and Paddling

There are four public use cabins on Nancy Lake, as well as many private ones. Three of the four public use cabins are about a half-mile walk down a leafy, gated gravel road from the trailhead at mile 1.8 of the Nancy Lake Parkway. Cabin 4 is the largest of the cabins, with room to sleep eight, plus a large covered porch. Cabin 3 is only accessible by boat since it is surrounded by private property.

There is also a put-in at the lake a few hundred yards before the parking area, with a short portage to the put-in on the lakeshore. Tippecanoe Rentals stores their boats by the road. You can load cabin camping gear into the boat and easily float it around to the cabins while other people in the party walk the trail unencumbered by stuff.

To eliminate that short portage, another put-in option for Nancy Lake is at the Nancy Lake Boat Launch off Buckingham Palace Road. There is a ramp for launching trailered boats and just a short walk across the beach for a paddler loading a canoe. It is a little longer paddle through the more developed portion on Nancy Lake to reach the public use cabins, but it can be a good option if you have a lot of loose gear.

The quick and easy access, plentiful cabins, and flatwater make Nancy Lake ideally suited for families with young children, less experienced campers, or large groups. There are many private cabins on the lake, but only a few are directly visible from the public use cabins, giving some sense of isolation. This is not really a wilderness trip but more of a pleasant weekend among the trees. Using a cabin as a base camp and setting out on meandering paddles around the lake is a great way for beginning boaters to practice and build confidence.

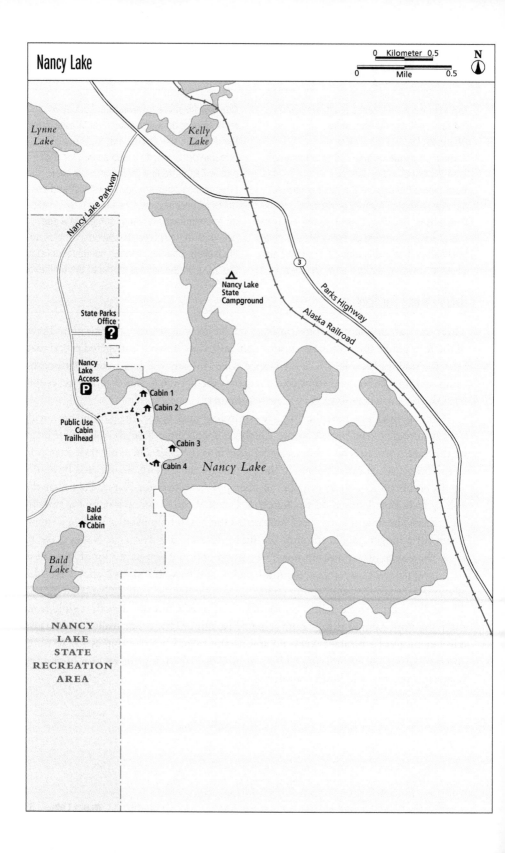

15 Tanaina Lake Canoe Loop Trail

Trip summary: A pleasant introduction to portage trails.
Distance: Approximately 13 miles of paddling and portaging.
Estimated paddling time: Allow 2 days for the loop, longer for free-form exploration.
Boat types: Canoe capable of being easily carried over trails.
Special features: Gentle lake paddle with portage trails.
Difficulties: Advanced beginner. Class I, wind can create waves on the larger lakes.
Season: Late May through early October.

Contact for more information: For cabin reservations and general area information, do a web search for "Alaska State Parks, Nancy Lake Recreation Area." For canoe rental information, do a web search for "Tippecanoe Rental" to find their phone number. Tippecanoe does not have a website and conducts all business over the phone. You make an appointment with them to meet at a specific time at Rolly Lake Campground to pick up life jackets, paddles, and the combination(s) to the locks on the canoes stored at the trailhead.

Overview

The loop of lakes and portage trails is the main attraction of the Nancy Lake State Recreation Area. The portages between the lakes are extremely well maintained, with boardwalks over swampy sections, informative signs, and outhouses at the designated camping areas. There are a number of public use cabins throughout the lake system. There are plenty of established places to camp overnight, and there is no need to camp in virgin spots.

The longest portage between lakes is 0.3 miles, with most portages considerably shorter. However, many people have not encountered portage trails before and become discouraged after one outing. A little thought and preparation for the special circumstances of combining hiking with paddling will go a long way toward making these trails fun.

First, your boat must be easy for one person to carry—two people on a boat is just plain awkward. At home, swing the boat onto your shoulders and see how it feels. If it's too heavy and/or clumsy to carry for 20 minutes, consider getting a boat that is easy to carry. On the Nancy Lake system, wheeled carts for carrying boats are allowed, but duckboards, narrow bumpy trails, and wet spots render them unpractical.

Second, think through your gear. If one person carries the camping gear in a pack and the other person the boat, you only have to walk the portage once. An extra load makes the portage three times as long since you have to double back to retrieve it. The system works best if the boat carrier wears their life jacket as a shoulder pad with the light, bulky gear in a pack, and the other person carries the heavy backpack and paddles.

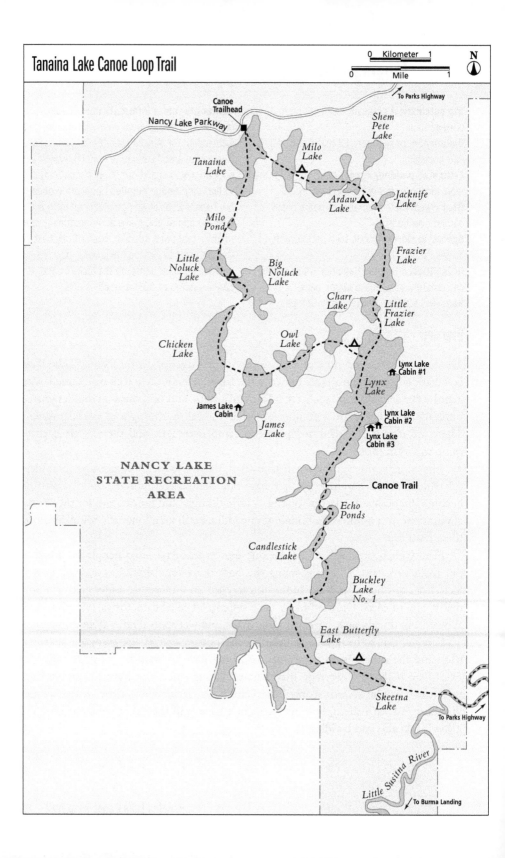

Tanaina Lake Canoe Loop Trail

0 Kilometer 1
0 Mile 1

N

To Parks Highway

Canoe Trailhead

Nancy Lake Parkway

Shem Pete Lake

Milo Lake

Tanaina Lake

Ardaw Lake

Jacknife Lake

Milo Pond

Frazier Lake

Little Noluck Lake

Big Noluck Lake

Charr Lake

Little Frazier Lake

Chicken Lake

Owl Lake

Lynx Lake Cabin #1

Lynx Lake

James Lake Cabin

Lynx Lake Cabin #2

Lynx Lake Cabin #3

James Lake

NANCY LAKE STATE RECREATION AREA

Canoe Trail

Echo Ponds

Candlestick Lake

Buckley Lake No. 1

East Butterfly Lake

Skeetna Lake

To Parks Highway

Little Susitna River

To Burma Landing

The Paddling

Park at the Tanaina Loop canoe trailhead, mile 4.7 on Nancy Lake Parkway. Tippecanoe Rentals stores boats here, too.

Most travelers begin the loop heading east—and this discussion will also—since this is the shortest distance to the first camp spot at the west end of Ardaw Lake. Just a roughly 30-minute paddle and portage from the Tanaina Loop trailhead, the west end campsite is the most heavily used in the Nancy Lake system. There is not great fishing in Ardaw Lake, but it is a pretty spot. Like all the official tenting sites on the Tanaina Loop, there are fire rings, an outhouse, and a large steel bear box. If the west end tent site is occupied, paddle across Ardaw Lake and there is another, less used tenting site at the portage trail on the east side.

Lynx Lake, at the head of the loop, has three public use cabins, as well as a large tenting area. They are usually the easiest cabins to get a reservation for during peak use times. The tenting area can handle up to five small groups and has an outhouse.

There are a number of private cabins on this lake, as well as a small summer camp. A private, gated road leads to this lake, and homeowners can drive here. Float planes may also land. Therefore, despite being relatively far into the trail system, Lynx Lake can get busy on holiday weekends.

Lynx is also a large lake, almost 2 miles long. When the wind starts blowing, the waves can get large.

The canoe trail splits at Lynx Lake. One arm leads south as far as the banks of the Little Susitna River. The trail is considerably less used and maintained than the loop, although Butterfly Lake has a number of private cabins since the southern shore of the lake defines the boundary of the state recreation area. Some cabin owners have float planes, so don't be shocked to see planes landing or taking off from the water on Butterfly.

There is a small, lightly used tenting area and outhouse on the north shore of Skeetna Lake. The trail from Skeetna Lake to Little Susitna River is a little narrow and swampy with more deadfall trees than Tanaina Loop portage trails. Roughly 0.5 miles, it is the longest portage in the Nancy Lake Canoe Trails system. It is possible to float the Little Susitna River to the takeout at Burma Landing. That trip is discussed in detail in the Little Susitna River chapter of this guide (chapter 13).

Heading west on the canoe loop from Lynx Lake completes the journey back to the trailhead. The cabin on James Lake is the most isolated of any cabin in the Nancy Lake State Recreation Area, since there is no mechanized way to get there in the summer. Official maps show a multiuse trail from James Lake with a portage and connecting float down Lynx Creek back to Lynx Lake. The portage trail is not consistently maintained for summer walking, and the route is not a practical one for most paddlers.

The tenting area between Big Noluck and Little Noluck lakes is the only other established overnight spot before the trailhead, with room for two small groups.

16 South Rolly Lake and Campground

Character: A small, stocked lake at the end of Nancy Lake Parkway. A pleasant campground lines the shore, with canoe rentals available, permitting paddling throughout the day.

Lake size: Roughly 0.25 miles by 0.25 miles.

Boat types: Anything that floats.

Special features: Shoreline boat rental and campground. Only electric motors are permitted on the lake.

Difficulties: Beginner. Class I, minor wind potential.

Season: Late May through October.

Contact for more information: For cabin reservations and general area information, do a web search for "Alaska State Parks, Nancy Lakes Recreation Area." For canoe rental information, do a web search for "Tippecanoe Rental" to find their phone number. Tippecanoe does not have a website and conducts all business over the phone. You make an appointment with them to meet at a specific time at Rolly Lake campground to pick up life jackets, paddles, and the combination(s) to the locks on the canoes stored at the trailhead.

South Rolly Lake and Campground offers a pleasant combination of car camping and paddling.

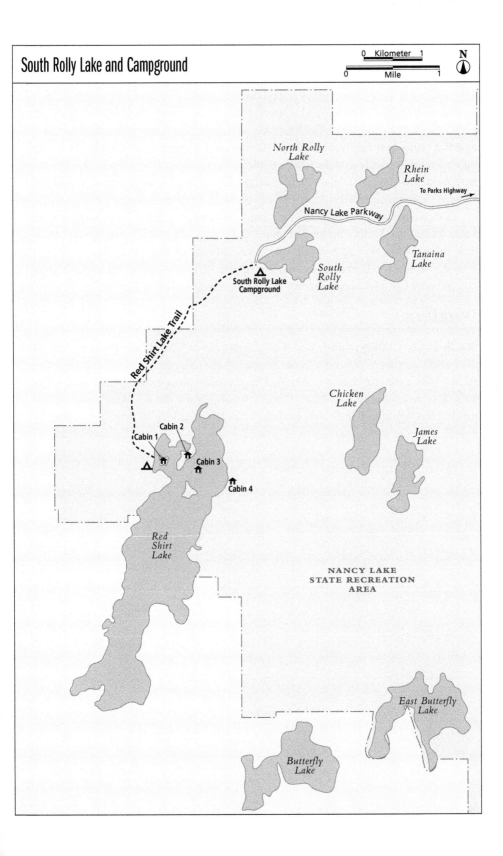

South Rolly Lake and Campground

Overview and Paddling

The combination of a quiet, tree-shaded campground on the southwest shore, canoe rentals, and an end-of-the-road location, makes South Rolly Lake quite a pleasant paddle. With the exception of holidays and warm weekends, it can be relatively easy to get a camp spot on shore. Online reservations for camp spots can also be made up to 7 months in advance for Alaska residents, and 6 months in advance for out-of-state residents. The lake is stocked, so fishing can be decent. Only electric motors are allowed on the lake, and it is tranquil.

The lake is a delightful paddle. Hopefully, you can get a shore-side camping spot. Launch the boat. Lazily explore the shore. On a warm day, hop in for a swim. Do a little fishing. Mess around. South Rolly Lake is fun for all ages.

The trailhead to Red Shirt Lake is just opposite the entrance to the campground, and the walk can provide alternative recreation throughout your stay.

General Access

South Rolly Campground: Located 6.2 miles down Nancy Lake Parkway (which heads west at mile 67.3 on the Parks Highway), the campground is operated by the Alaska State Parks contractor and staffed by caretakers in summer. Tippecanoe keeps a stock of rental canoes on shore. If you are parking for the day, Alaska State Parks parking fees apply, and your annual Alaska State Parks parking sticker is valid here.

17 Red Shirt Lake

Trip summary: An easy hike to a large lake with a number of public use and private cabins.
Distance: Approximately 3 miles hiking, with at most a 0.75-mile paddle across the lake to the farthest public use cabin.
Estimated paddling time: Allow 2 hours for the hike, then another hour to transfer gear to a canoe and paddle to a cabin.
Boat types: Rental canoe.
Special features: A hike down a well-maintained trail to a lake with cabins.
Difficulties: Advanced beginner. Class I, although wind can create waves.

Season: Late May through early October.
Contact for more information: For cabin reservations and general area information, do a web search for "Alaska State Parks, Nancy Lake Recreation Area." For canoe rental information, do a web search for "Tippecanoe Rental" to find their phone number. Tippecanoe does not have a website and conducts all business over the phone. You make an appointment with them to meet at a specific time at Rolly Lake campground to pick up life jackets, paddles, and the combination(s) to the locks on the canoes stored at the trailhead.

Overview

A pleasant hiking trail over moraines leads from the parking lot to Red Shirt Lake. This trail makes a great first overnight backpack trip for small children. Tippecanoe Rentals has canoes for rent already at the lakeshore, sparing you an epic portage. Red Shirt Lake itself is more than 3 miles long, with a number of interesting nooks to explore. There is a well-maintained camping area at the end of the hiking trail on the lake shore. There are also four public use cabins for rent from Alaska State Parks, which are all a short paddle from the hiking trailhead. Over half of the lakeshore is private property, and there are a number of private residences.

General Access

Park at the South Rolly Lake parking area, mile 6.6 of the Nancy Lake Parkway. Alaska State Parks parking fees apply and your annual Alaska State Parks parking sticker is valid here.

The Hike and Paddle

A 3-mile walk over a rolling moraine follows a well-maintained trail from the trailhead to Red Shirt Lake. Tippecanoe Rentals has a number of canoes locked and chained at the lakeshore; make rental arrangements with them before leaving for the trip, preferably at the same time you make the cabin reservation, which should be months in advance for summertime weekends and holidays. It is a quick paddle from the trailhead to any of the cabins, but leave plenty of time to unlock the canoe and transfer your packs to the boat.

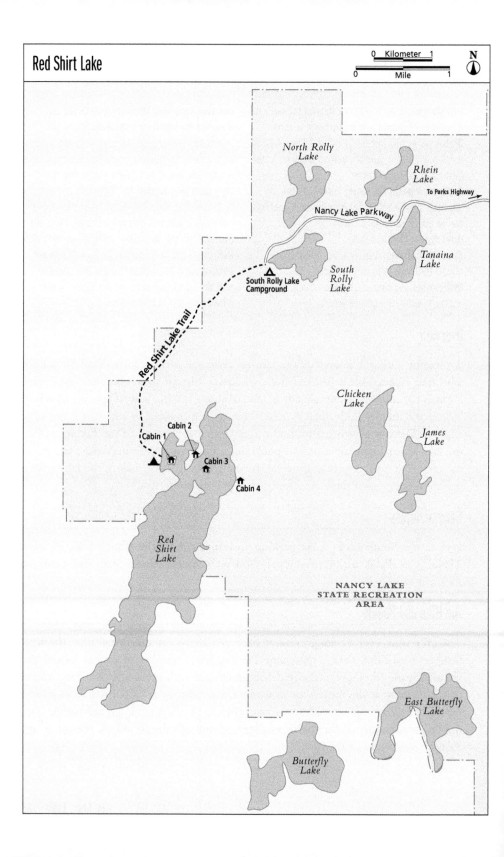

Red Shirt Lake is more than 3 miles long, and there are plenty of opportunities for open-ended exploring. Especially inviting are the numerous coves and inlets from tributary creeks. Fishing for pike can be good and there is a decent population of rainbow trout. Watch out for strong winds—they can churn large waves on the lake.

Please keep in mind that the southern two-thirds of the Red Shirt Lake is private property, so do not walk above the highwater line here.

18 Willow Creek and Susitna River–Parks Highway to Deshka Landing

Character: Great fishing on a tightly winding, tree-obstructed clearwater creek.

Distance: 4.75 miles on Willow Creek from the Parks Highway to the Susitna River, a further 4.5 miles on the Susitna River to Deshka Landing.

Estimated paddling time: Paddling time is highly dependent on water level, obstructing trees in the channel, boat type, and paddler skill. A small kayak can paddle down Willow Creek in 1.5 hours and then take an additional 0.75 hours to get to Deshka Landing on the Susitna River. A small cataraft, rowed steadily with no fishing, can take 4 to 5 hours on Willow Creek and a further 2 hours to Deshka Landing. Allow additional time earlier in the spring for more obstructions on the channel to portage around. Allow more time at low water for more dragging through shallows.

Boat types: Small cataraft with open floor, or small kayak with large cockpit opening.

Special features: Great fishing, clear water, lots of campsites.

Difficulties: Intermediate. Class II, snags, sweepers, strainers, trees completely obstructing channel, tight beds, shallow water, fast current, flying hooks from combat fishing, airboats.

Season: Late May through the end of September.

Contact for more information: For general information and campsite reservations, do a web search for "Alaska State Parks Willow Creek Recreation Area."

Overview

Willow Creek is a wildly popular fishing spot. Some years, the road-accessible clear water of the creek hosts a thick king salmon run. Almost all boats on the creek are fishing boats. It is so well loved that salmon fishing is restricted to weekends for most of the summer. A close reading of the minutely detailed and constantly evolving fishing regulations is a must before putting into this water.

When king salmon fishing is open, the creek is a zoo. Airboats blast up and down the narrow channel. Lines of catarafts bump through holes. Combat fishing fills the banks. A float at that time is a utilitarian search for fish.

However, the creek is surprisingly empty when salmon fishing is not allowed. There will be almost no other boats or people. And there are other kinds of fish to go for as well. Almost every bend of the river is sandy and ideal for camping.

You need excellent boat control to float this creek. The smaller the cataraft, the easier the float will be, since many gaps between obstacles are only a few feet wide and dragging through shallows or around obstacles will be easier. An open floor on the cataraft makes it easier to push through shallows. A short kayak with a large cockpit opening, making it easier to enter and exit the boat, is the fastest craft on the water without a motor. However, it is harder to fish from a kayak, so rafts dominate the paddled fleet.

A float down Willow Creek can feel like a trip through trees more than a paddle on water.

All this said, floating Willow Creek is one heck of a lot of fun. Try it sometime when salmon fishing isn't open. It makes a nice mid-week run just for a great thing to do on a summer day.

General Access

Put-in: From the Parks Highway, mile 71.4, there are two private campgrounds on either side of the creek. Parking and boat launch fees apply.

Takeout: Willow Creek State Recreation Area and Campground. From mile 70.8 on the Parks Highway, turn west on Willow Creek Parkway and follow it 3.7 miles to the end. Alaska State Parks parking fees apply, and your annual Alaska State Parks parking sticker is valid here. There is no boat launch here. You have to carry your boat

Willow Creek and Susitna River–Parks Highway to Deshka Landing

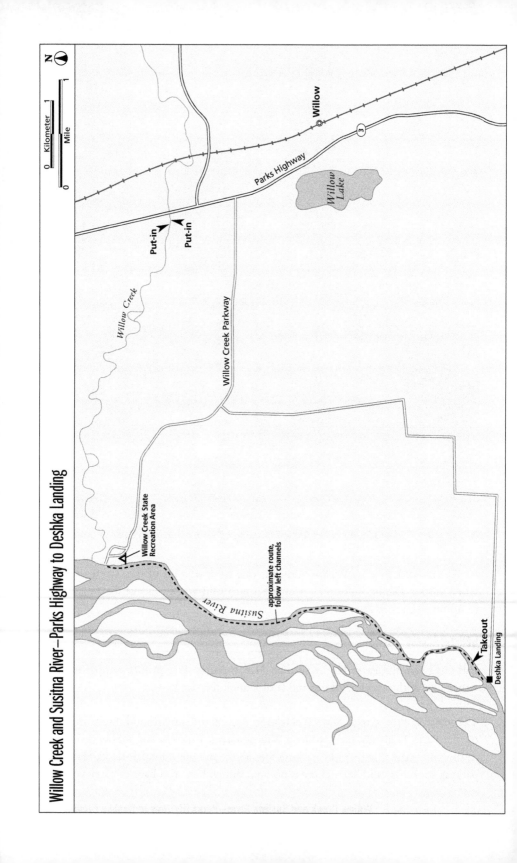

from shore to the vehicle at the day use parking lot, almost 0.25 miles. Therefore, it is only suitable for small, light craft. Walk to the beach to get a good look at the take-out before floating. Some years, there is a concessionaire renting rafts and providing shuttles from the day use parking lot. If floating with two people, one can watch the gear, while the other bikes the 5 miles back to the highway put-in.

Alternate takeout: Deshka Landing. If you have a trailered boat with lots of gear, Deshka Landing is the nearest boat launch downstream from the Willow Creek mouth. It is privately operated and open 24 hours a day in the summer. A credit card pays for the automatic gate to open. To get there, turn onto Willow Creek Parkway as described above, then follow the signs to Deshka Landing.

The Paddling

Willow Creek conditions are constantly changing. Original channel reading and obstacle avoidance will be necessary at all times. It is a challenging float. (Anchorage paddlers will find it to be sort of like Campbell Creek, but bigger, faster, and with more trees in the water.) It is best done on warm, sunny days because you will probably get wet. Trees are in the channel the entire length of the creek, sometimes completely blocking the water, creating sweepers, strong eddies, and presenting an almost perpetual obstacle. Hold to the inside of bends to encounter fewer overhanging trees and allow more time to scan the water ahead. Stop and scout blind corners. Given a choice between a shallow channel and one filled with trees, pick the shallow channel: dragging over gravel is much easier and safer than a sweeper entanglement. All other factors being equal, there tend to be fewer trees in the channel later in the summer as people chainsaw the worst obstacles. Keep in mind, however, that the channel is always changing and trees are continually falling in the water. Always, always be scanning ahead.

When king salmon fishing is open, crowd management skills become necessary, too. Airboats are a real hazard; it is hard to believe people cram such big boats down such a small, tree-choked channel. Pull over to the bank when you hear one coming. If people are fishing in the water, try to pass behind them, away from the hole, and tell them what you are doing so they do not backcast. If given the opportunity, swing wide of the bank fishermen beyond the farthest possible cast.

Willow Creek ends at the fast, silty water of the Susitna River. Willow Creek Campground is on the left bank at the mouth. If you don't see hordes of fishermen, you will see the trampled trails. The best small boat access is at the end of the bank fishing, actually on the Susitna River.

If floating down to Deshka Landing, stick to the left bank of the Susitna. The channel frays many times, but stick to the left. Deshka Landing is just in front of the high silt bluffs. Watch for weird eddies at the point of the jetty.

19 Talkeetna Lakes Park

Character: Medium-sized lakes with good fishing, foot path access, and portage trails.
Lake size: Varies from 1,000 to 3,000 feet long.
Boat types: Any boat that is easy to carry for 100 yards.
Special features: Good fishing. Great walking trail system surrounding the lakes. Excellent portage trails. Well-maintained area.

Difficulties: Beginner. Class I, wind is not a problem.
Season: Late May through October.
Contact for more information: For stocking information, do a web search for "Alaska Department of Fish and Game Mat Su stocking."

Overview

The town of Talkeetna sits at the end of the dead-end Talkeetna Spur Road off mile 98.7 of the Parks Highway. Originally a railroad town, its primary industry, now, is catering to Denali mountain climbers and other tourists. Set in the broad, glacial outwash of the Susitna River valley, there are numerous small lakes between the gravel ridges. It feels like northern Wisconsin or Minnesota, but with mountain peaks in the distance.

Talkeetna Lakes Park, just south of the Talkeetna town center, is a well-maintained water and land trail system. Wide, smooth paths loops around and between the lakes. The paths are great for walking or biking in the summer and are groomed for cross-country skiing in the winter. Additionally, there are well-marked portage trails leading directly from lake to lake. These small- to medium-sized lakes, well connected by land, are great for pleasant paddling, swimming, or fishing for stocked trout.

General Access

X Lake access (Comsat trailhead): At mile 12 of the Talkeetna Spur Road, turn east onto Comsat Road. Roughly 500 feet later, turn into the gravel parking lot. This is the main parking lot for the park. There is a pit toilet and information board. The daily parking fee is $5 and payable to the Mat-Su Borough. Alaska State Parks annual parking passes aren't valid here. It is an easy 0.1-mile portage from the parking to the lake—the road is smooth, even a wheeled cart would work to carry the boat. There is a dock on the beach to aid launching.

Y Lake access: This is an informal, unmarked access. Keep driving on Comcast Road past the Christiansen Lake Road intersection. Shortly, a guardrail appears on the right with a small gravel parking area at the end of it. A short, steep portage trail leads down to a good launching beach on Y Lake. Although there is no direct parking fee here, please pay at the X Lake trailhead or have a Mat-Su annual pass to contribute your portion to trail maintenance.

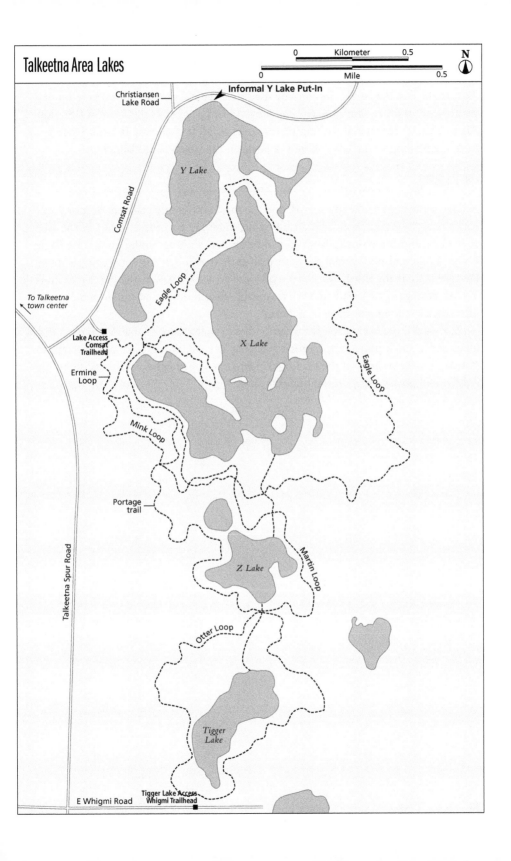

Tigger Lake access (Whigmi trailhead): At mile 10.8 of the Talkeetna Spur Road, turn east on Whigmi Road. This parking area is the southern entrance to the Talkeetna Lakes Park and is less heavily used than the X Lake entrance. There is not a permanent pit toilet. The daily parking fee is $5 and payable to the Mat-Su Borough. Alaska State Parks annual parking passes aren't valid. It is an easy 0.1-miles portage from the parking to the lake. There is a dock on the beach to aid launching.

The Paddling

X Lake is the largest lake in the park and the most commonly paddled. At more than half a mile long and about half a mile wide, there are two major lobes of the lake to explore, and three small islands to paddle around. Fishing can be good. The Eagle Loop hiking and biking trail has informal spurs that touch the southeastern shore. Portage trails at the north and south ends lead to other lakes in the park. The short Y Lake portage is well marked, with reasonably firm footing, and is used much more often than the longer portage to Z Lake.

Y, Z, and Tigger Lakes are all smaller bodies of water than X Lake. Y Lake has two lobes and a quick portage to Comsat Road or Z Lake. The Z Lake portage trail to X Lake is quite swampy at the landing. Tigger Lake is a straightforward paddle to the lightly used portage trail on the opposite shore.

20 East and Middle Forks of the Chulitna and Chulitna Rivers

Character: Road-accessible floating through Denali State Park. Variety of water character and doable rapids.

Distance: Approximately 10 miles on the Forks, then 33 miles on the Chulitna River. Allow 3 days for a comfortable float.

Estimated paddling time: Roughly 16 hours of paddling time. Allow 3 days for a comfortable float including shuttling.

Boat types: Small cataraft or small kayak.

Special features: On clear days, great views of Denali, varied channel types, abundant wildlife.

Difficulties: Intermediate. Tight narrow channel on the Forks has sweepers, snag, and shallows. The main Chuitna has Class II to III water and braided sections. Brown bears sometimes fish while standing in the channel.

Contact for more information: For general information and campsite reservations, do a web search for "Alaska State Parks Denali State Park."

Overview

On a clear day, the glaciers and mountains leading to Denali tower over the west side of the valley. There is a range of channel and water types. The float starts on a narrow, clear creek with some tree dodging and Class II rapids. The Chulitna itself is a glacier fed river. On the upper portion, there are steep walled cliffs with boiling eddies and wave trains along the base. On the lower portion the channel becomes braided.

The Chulitna is a salmon-bearing stream. And bears like salmon. When the fish are running, you are likely to see at least a few feeding in the water.

General Access

Put-in: Parks Highway, mile 185. There are no signs for a put-in, but there are numerous clear gravel bars down to the bank. The south side of the bridge is generally the more accessible side to put-in. Some years AK DOT grades the gravel into a berm too vertical for many vehicles to drive over, but generally you can back a trailer to the water.

Takeout: Parks Highway, mile 133. This is informally called the "The Princess Hotel Bridge." There are no signs for the takeout. The gravel road is northwest of the bridge, on the opposite side of the road from the Princess access, and within sight of the mile 133 marker. There is a lockable gate at top of the road, but it has been years since it has been locked. It is a steep drive down to the water and sometimes the beach is narrow. It is worth scouting the drive before taking your vehicle and trailer down it. And once near the water, take a few moments to scout the takeout before putting-in upriver. Many people park their shuttle vehicles up by the highway rather than leave them down low by the river.

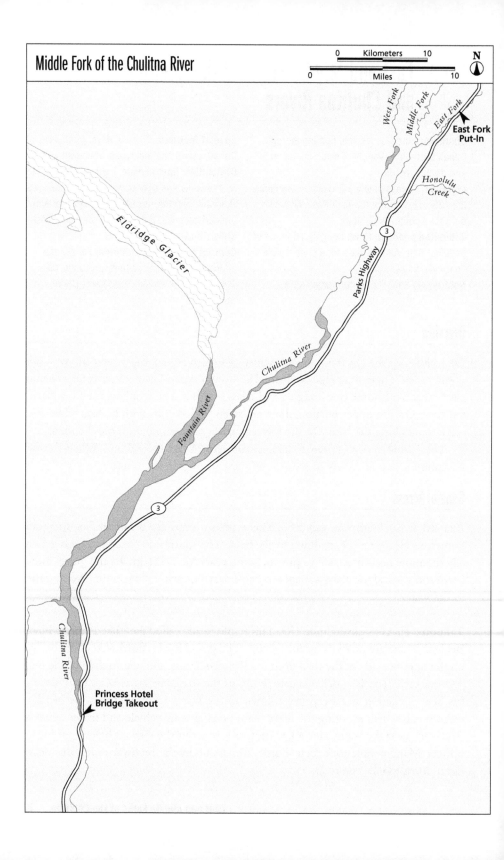

Middle Fork of the Chulitna River

Kilometers 0 — 10

Miles 0 — 10

N

West Fork

Middle Fork

East Fork

East Fork Put-In

Honolulu Creek

Eldridge Glacier

Parks Highway

Chulitna River

Fountain River

3

3

Chulitna River

Princess Hotel Bridge Takeout

The Paddling

Put in on the East Fork. The East Fork begins as a small channel with clear water. It is narrow enough that trees are a definite hazard. There will be some sweepers and probably a blocked channel or two. Scout blind turns as much as possible.

Roughly 2 hours into the float the channel narrows and Class II to III rock-dodging rapids begin. As you float under the railroad bridge, the rapids pick up intensity with the addition of the Middle Fork of the Chulitna from the right. If you are in a raft or capable kayak, the rapids are fun. They continue all the way to the mouth of Honolulu Creek.

Signaling the approach to the Honolulu Creek, the railroad comes close to the left bank a bend or so above the mouth. Honolulu is a king salmon stream. There is an ATV trail from the Parks Highway to the mouth. With a packraft, it possible to walk out and end the trip here. In years where King salmon fishing is allowed, fishing is open on weekends. Bears fish 7 days a week. It is not a good place to camp.

Just after Honolulu Creek, the West Fork of the Chulitna joins the flow to make the official mainstem Chulitna River. The water will be silty from now on.

The channel is now wider. Sheer rock walls sometimes line the shore and there are Class II to III wave trains and turbulence along the bases. The rock walls appear intermittently until the Fountain River enters from the right and the channel becomes heavily braided.

The braids are relatively straight forward for experienced Alaska paddlers to navigate. The gravel bars make excellent camp sites; just stick to the middle of the river and away from the mouths of clearwater streams since that is where the salmon and bears are.

Roughly two miles above the takeout, the channel consolidates into one unbroken stretch of water. Line up on the left when the bridge comes into sight for the takeout.

It is possible to keep paddling down the Chulitna to the town of Talkeetna. Scout the takeout in Talkeetna in advance of putting in since there is no formal takeout there and the channel constantly changes. A more reliable takeout is to continue floating past Talkeetna and onto the Susitna. Takeout on the right on the gravel bars—unofficially called "Sunshine"—just after the Parks Highway bridge. Allow an additional day to go from the Princess Bridge to Sunshine.

III. Kenai Peninsula

The Kenai Peninsula is perhaps one of the best loved, and most heavily used, recreational playgrounds in Alaska. Its spectacular scenery and water, relatively easy road access, and proximity to Anchorage all combine to attract lots of people.

Kenai Peninsula

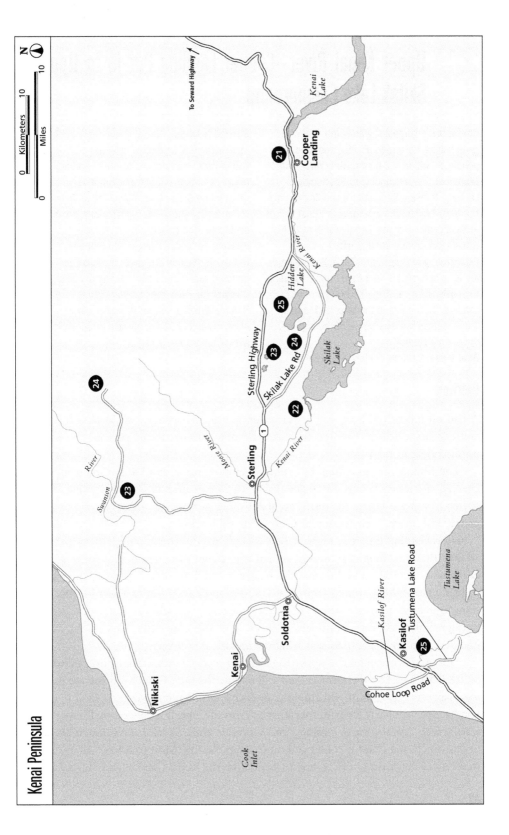

21 Upper Kenai River–Cooper Landing Put-in to Upper Skilak Lake Campground

Character: A gorgeous, glacial-fed river with great fishing, easy road access, and tons of people, all within a 2-hour drive of Anchorage.

Distance: Cooper Landing to Sportsman's Landing, 8 miles; Sportsman's Landing to Jim's Landing, 4 miles; Jim's Landing to Kenai mouth at Skilak Lake, 5 miles; Kenai mouth to Upper Skilak Lake Campground, 7 miles.

Estimated paddling time: (The following times are for a cataraft.) 1 hour from Cooper Landing to Sportsman's Landing, 0.5 hours to Jim's Landing, 0.75 hours to the lake, and roughly 1 hour across the lake with a 35-horsepower motor on a cataraft.

Boat types: Cataraft or plastic river kayak.

Special features: Glacial green water, spectacular scenery, incredible fishing.

Difficulties: Intermediate to Jim's Landing, advanced intermediate through the Kenai Canyon and Skilak Lake. Class II to III, frigid water, lots of people, flying fishhooks, bears accustomed to people.

Season: Early May through late October. (Although much of the upper river can be paddled year round when wearing dry suits.)

Contact for more information: Kenai National Wildlife Refuge: kenai.fws.gov; Alaska Fish and Game, Division of Sport Fish: www.sf.adfg.state.ak.us.

Overview

A ban on motorized boat traffic, fun water, spectacular scenery, world-class fishing, and easy road access combine to make the upper Kenai River perhaps the most paddled river in the state.

The fishing is outstanding: red salmon, rainbow trout, and Dolly Varden fill the channel, attracting hordes of anglers from Anchorage and all over the world. This stretch of water is where the term "combat fishing" was invented. At least one or two people lose an eye here every year from flying fishhooks.

However, that does not mean it isn't a lovely paddle worth doing. Many people arrange their paddling year around annual trips down this section. The water is just challenging enough to be fun, and the scenery is sublime. If your primary interest is paddling, not fishing, timing your float for May and early June, and again in the fall from September through the end of October, when major salmon runs aren't passing through, will make for a considerably more enjoyable experience. You might wet a line then, too, and be surprised at what the crowds are missing.

This guide concludes the upper Kenai River section with a description of upper Skilak Lake. The lake is enormous and will require the use of a motor if you are floating in any sort of a raft. It will also require excellent judgment and extra food in case you have to wait a day for better weather to cross the lake. It is dangerous: I have personally seen 20-foot waves crashing into shoreside cliffs. Skilak Lake is much like an ocean, except the water is colder and more unpredictable. Most paddlers will want to travel no farther than Jim's Landing to avoid both the Kenai Canyon and Skilak Lake.

Princess Rapids is fun, and it is the start of the nonmotorized portion of the upper Kenai River.

As a last note, the Alaska Department of Fish and Game begins their mile count on the Kenai River from the perspective of a returning salmon. So, the mouth is mile 0, counting up against the current. Since this river is so heavily fished, this guide follows the ADF&G mile count.

General Access

The Sterling Highway frequently intersects the upper Kenai River, creating a wealth of put-in and takeout options (by Alaska standards). The following list heads downriver.

Sterling Highway, mile 48.0, Cooper Landing put-in (a.k.a. the Kenai Lake Outlet put-in): Operated by Alaska State Parks, there is a boat launch and overnight parking for a fee.

Sterling Highway, mile 54.8, Russian River Ferry (a.k.a. Sportsman's Landing): A privately operated ferry carries fishermen across the Kenai to fishing at the Russian River mouth. The fee parking spaces here are usually overwhelmed within the vicinity of salmon runs.

Skilak Lake Road, 0.2 miles from the turnoff for the Sterling Highway at mile 58.0: Jim's Landing is a large gravel parking lot with no overnight parking operated by the Kenai National Wildlife Refuge. This is the last pull-out to a vehicle before the Class III water of the Kenai Canyon and the potentially dangerous water of Skilak Lake.

Skilak Road, mile 8.5 Upper Skilak Lake Campground: Operated by the Bureau of Land Management, overnight parking is free in the numerous gravel parking spots.

There are commercial shuttle services that will move your vehicles and/or pick your boat up. Do a web search for "Kenai River shuttle" and make follow-up calls to choose one.

The Paddling

From the Cooper Landing put-in at the Kenai Lake outlet: The slackwater ends just above Princess Rapids at river mile 80. Just above the rapids a power line crosses the river and a sign on shore clearly states that motorboats are not allowed downriver of that point. Princess Rapids is Class II to III, with large standing waves and some rocks in the wide channel, but the run is short and easy to scout from the water. Below the rapids there are other, smaller rapids, along with numerous gravel bars and occasional islands, depending on water level. The best fishing will be where clear, flowing tributaries enter the green Kenai. Many people set up camp on the islands.

The next large rapids are at Schooner Bend, river mile 76, at the bend after passing under the Sterling Highway bridge. This Class III section can have quite large standing waves. Watch for Preacher Rock and the hole behind it at the end of the wave train; pull hard right after the waves to avoid it. The waves are a lot of fun (usually) to run in a raft but are certainly too much for an inexperienced boater. Stick to the inside of the bend to travel through smoother water.

Around a mile or so from the rapids during salmon season, crowds of fishermen will start appearing on the banks, especially the left one. They are all there to fish the mouth of the Russian River. This clearwater tributary has thick runs of red salmon. Stick to the right channel to avoid passing by the mouth (hidden by the dividing island) and the thicket of flying fishhooks and weights. Watch for brown bears along the banks here and do not leave any food or fish unattended if you pull over to shore. In a boat, bears will not be a problem.

The parking lot just above the ferry cable is Sportsman's Landing (also called the Russian River Ferry parking). When it is not fishing season and overflowing, the parking lot can be a good takeout to end a short float, which should take around an hour of steady paddling. There is a developed boat launch here, too.

Many people continue on another 3.5 river miles to Jim's Landing. There are no rapids on this section of the upper Kenai, and fewer gravel bars, but there are many

Upper Kenai River—Cooper Landing Put-in to Upper Skilak Lake Campground

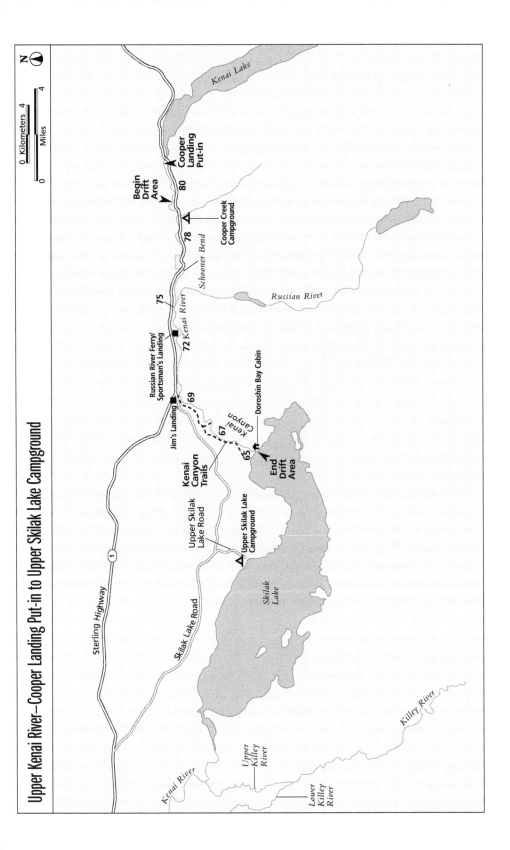

excellent fishing holes and established, but unofficial, camping spots. Line up on the right side of the bank when you spot the landing. The short beach is right in front of the point on a gravel bar. This is the last boat takeout before the Class III (IV at high water) rapids of Kenai Canyon, and you must pull over here if you don't want to run the canyon. (There is a foot trail that parallels the right bank on the upper 2 miles of the canyon if you need to leave in an emergency, but there are no more boat pull-outs).

The Kenai Canyon has large standing waves and boulders. It is best run in a cataraft by experienced, alert boaters. It is also run by experienced, knowledgeable boaters in drift boats. If running it in a river kayak, your skills must be excellent since waves will likely break over your head. Once you start to float the canyon, you are committed. You can scout the water from the hiking trails that parallel the canyon before putting-in. Park at the clearly marked and developed trailheads on Skilak Lake Road, then walk to scout the canyon if it will be your first time running it. Once you are in the canyon, visibility of upcoming water tends to be good if you are sitting high on a raft. The canyons last for 2 miles and can be quite a good, cold thrill.

The river slows and breaks into many small channels as it enters the still water of Skilak Lake. Follow the left fork to Doroshin Bay. The Kenai National Wildlife Refuge operates the Doroshin Bay Cabin, a four-person public use cabin available by reservation. The trail to the cabin can be difficult to spot from a boat, so the GPS coordinates of the cabin can be handy: N60.42622' / W150.14062'.

Follow channels to the right to head directly toward the takeout at the Upper Skilak Campground. Lots of very large bears congregate where the Kenai River enters Skilak Lake, especially by the sloughs where Hidden Creek enters. Tent camping here is not a good idea.

The water of Skilak Lake is dangerous. Winds can pick up suddenly, churning enormous waves. If you capsize on the lake, you will probably get hypothermia and drown. Do not head out on the lake if it is windy. It can be a wiser choice to beach the boat and walk up the Hidden Lake trail, then return in the calmer air of morning. Motors are allowed on the lake, and if you have a raft or drift boat, you will want to use it. Try to stick as close to shore as possible, but don't go between the island and the cliffs on the point during rough weather.

22 Middle Kenai River–Lower Skilak Lake Campground to Bing's Landing

Character: A short lake paddle, followed by a float on a medium-sized river with outstanding fishing.

Distance: 12 water miles between the campground and Bing's Landing.

Estimated paddling time: Roughly 5 to 6 hours in a cataraft or rowed drift boat, 3 hours in a kayak.

Boat types: Drift boat, cataraft, or river kayak. (Canoes are marginal and not recommended.)

Special features: Large glacial lake, outlet channel, which can be paddled down and up! Incredible fishing.

Difficulties: Intermediate. Class I to II. Skilak Lake is unpredictable, frigid water. Motorboat traffic can render the Kenai unpaddlable in fishing season.

Season: Late May through October.

Contact for more information: For fishing information and regulations, do a web search for "Alaska Department of Fish and Game Kenai River." For campground reservation, do a web search for "Kenai National Wildlife Refuge Lower Skilak Lake Campground." For Bing's Landing information, do a web search for "Alaska State Park Bing's Landing."

Overview

The middle Kenai River has phenomenal fishing, especially for king and red salmon, plus trophy rainbow trout and Dolly Varden. The channel is scenic, too, with the glacial green water flowing between forested hills.

All these attractions render this section of the Kenai in danger of being loved to death. Numerous homes and lodges line the banks. Speeding motorboats throw high wakes. Fishing pressure, although mostly from boats, is intense. It is not a float through pristine wilderness.

However, the middle Kenai River is closed to motorized boats from March 15 through June 14, from the Skilak Lake outlet to the end of the first bend, or, as ADF&G defines it, from river 50 to 48. This is to allow fish a chance to spawn without heavy boat traffic. Late May and early June is an outstanding time to paddle, camp, and fish this section in relative seclusion. The current is slack enough that strong paddlers in kayaks can go down, then paddle back up the river, fishing the outlet hole repeatedly. Since the outlet hole is Kenai National Wildlife Refuge land and, therefore, public, camping is allowed on shore and there are numerous established but informal camping spots. An out-and-back paddle from Lower Skilak Lake Campground to the outlet hole is a pleasant way to inaugurate the summer paddling season—although you have to exercise weather judgment when crossing Skilak Lake.

Paddlers are further accommodated by "Motorless Mondays" in May, June, and July. On these days, fishing is not allowed from boats with motors from the lake outlet all the way to the mouth of the river. This all but eliminates motorized traffic and is a wonderful time to enjoy the river and some fishing.

The outlet of Skilak Lake not only has great fishing, but is one of the more lovely spots in the world.

As you are probably beginning to realize, there are so many users of the Kenai that regulations are necessary to accommodate them. A detailed perusal of the latest fishing regulations, which describe the boating restrictions, as well as reading signs posted at major access points, makes worthwhile research before floating this section of the river.

As a last note, the Alaska Department of Fish and Game begins their mile count on the Kenai River from the perspective of a returning salmon. So, the mouth is mile 0, counting up against the current. Since this river is so heavily fished, this guide follows the ADF&G mile count.

General Access

Put-in at Lower Skilak Lake Campground: To get to the campground, turn onto Skilak Lake Road from mile 75.3 on the Sterling Highway. (The sign indicating the turnoff to Skilak Lake Road is not always posted on both sides of the road, so pay attention to the mile markers to find the turn.) Drive 5.3 miles on the gravel Skilak Lake Road, then turn right at the well-signed turn to the campground. Operated by the Kenai National Wildlife Refuge, there is a boat launch here, lots of parking, as well as a number of pleasant campsites on the lakeshore. The launch can get quite

Middle Kenai River–Lower Skilak Lake Campground to Bing's Landing

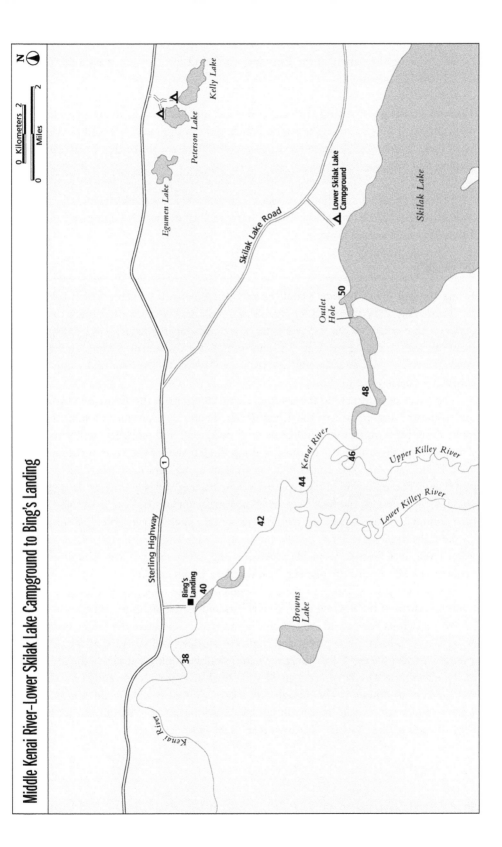

crowded during the height of the fishing season. Vandalism has not been a problem for vehicles left overnight.

Takeout at Bing's Landing: Turnoff at the well-marked road from Sterling Highway, mile 80.3. Bing's Landing is a boat launch and campground, operated by Alaska State Parks and staffed in season by a caretaker. There are reasonable boat launch, parking, and camping fees.

There are commercial shuttle services that will move your vehicles and/or pick your boat up. Type "Kenai River shuttle" into an Internet search engine and make follow-up calls to choose one.

The Paddling

From the put-in at Lower Skilak Lake Campground: Crossing Skilak Lake is not something to be taken lightly. Even this 1-mile paddle from the launch to the outlet can be tricky. Watch for wind-driven waves. Depending on wind direction, there can also be rolling swells to contend with, along with smaller whitecap waves. Fog can suddenly roll in, too, reducing visibility. Do not flip the boat under any circumstances. Stick close to shore.

The basalt boulders along the lakeshore mark the start of the inside bend to the outlet and the resumption of the Kenai River. There are a number of submerged rocks around this inside bend and boats with deep draft and propellers will want to swing wide of the inside; the channel is along the left side of the river at the outlet hole. There are numerous established informal camping sites on both sides of the outlet hole. The right side of the river has slower current and side sloughs. As long as you don't get too near the rocks and gravel bars at the end of the slack water, you can turn around and paddle back up the river reasonably easily in this hole. The sloughs on the right bank are easier to paddle up than the back eddy on the left, but at most water levels, it is possible to paddle upriver along either shore. If you find yourself unable to paddle against the current, float down to Bing's Landing.

Below river mile 49, stick to the left at the end of the outlet hole and begin the twists and turns of the flowing river. Gravel bars and islands are most common at the bends. Numerous houses and lodges dot the shore once you leave the refuge boundaries. If at all possible, give motorized skiffs the channel, and be wary of them. Pay attention to assorted signs describing regulations on the bank, especially at the mouth of the tributary Killey River. It is an 11-mile float from the lake to Bing's Landing, and the current flows quickly enough that a kayak should be able to do it in under 2 hours, and a raft or drift boat in almost twice as long if rowed steadily. Don't miss Bing's Landing. The Class III Naptown Rapids are below it.

Skilak Lake Area Lakes

Overview

The hills to the north of Skilak Lake are filled with many glacial remnant lakes. Found between the gravel Skilak Lake Road and the Sterling Highway, these lakes are easily accessible, scenic, and fun for the whole family. Managed by the federal Fish and Wildlife Service, a few of the lakes have public use cabins and boats available for rental, and others are connected by hiking trails. Many are stocked with rainbow trout for fishing. This diverse structure allows a wide range of activities, interests, and ages to converge and enjoy the water.

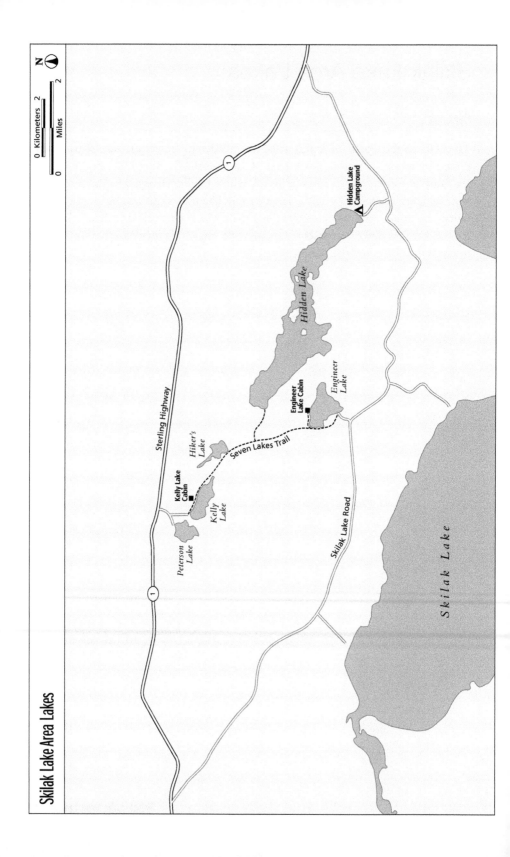

Skilak Lake Area Lakes

23 Kelly and Peterson Lakes

Character: Two small lakes with a small informal campground, a public use cabin that includes a rowboat, and a hiking trail. Great for families with children.

Lake size: Kelly Lake is roughly 0.75 miles long and 0.3 miles wide. Peterson Lake is much smaller and rounder, roughly one-third of a mile in diameter.

Boat types: Canoe, kayak, or rowboat.

Special features: Forgiving paddling, easy road access, a small campground, stocked fish, and an adjacent hiking trail. The Kelly Lake

Public Use Cabin is available for rent by reservation and comes with its own rowboat.

Difficulties: Beginner. Class I, cold water, occasional wind.

Season: Late May through October. (The lakes can have incredible ice-skating some winters.)

Contact for more information: For campground information and cabin reservations, including a rowboat, do a web search for "Kenai National Wildlife Refuge Kelly Lake."

Peterson Lake has easy access, camping, and plenty of flatwater to explore. It is fun for all ages and types.

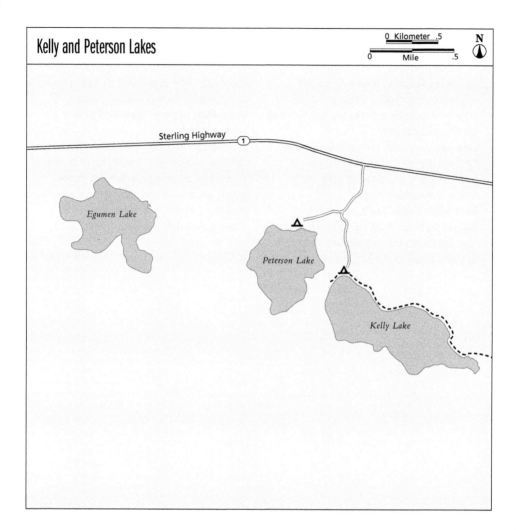

Kelly and Peterson Lakes

Sterling Highway

Egumen Lake

Peterson Lake

Kelly Lake

Overview

These two lakes are surprising little gems. The access is easy: just a short drive off the Sterling Highway, and you can even park within a few feet of shore to unload the boat from the car.

Kelly Lake has the larger campground and is a larger body of water, too. There is a public use cabin on the north shore, which is also accessible by trail or boat. Fishing for stocked rainbows in its numerous little coves can be good, especially so in the early spring and late fall.

The Seven Lakes hiking trail begins on the north shore. Although called "Seven Lakes," the hiking trail only connects four lakes. A quick 0.5 miles from the campground, the trail passes between the Kelly Lake public use cabin and its rowboat on the beach. Keep going on the trail to encounter Hikers Lake (more like a small pond), the northwestern end of Hidden Lake, and the terminus at Engineer Lake 4.4 miles from Kelly Lake.

In 2019, the Swan Lake fire burned through this area. The campground and cabin were successfully defended from the fire, but the surrounding taiga was scorched bare. In 2022, the mushrooms and fireweed are thick, and the views to the southern Kenai Mountains are charming. As brushy vegetation returns over the next 10 years, there should be an abundant moose population and other large animals attracted to the regrowth.

Peterson Lake is a smaller body of water and has fewer camping spots on shore. Therefore, it is less heavily used. It is a fine place to get a boat wet and putter around for some fishing and swimming—if it's warm.

General Access

Turn off at the Kelly/Peterson Lakes sign at mile 68.3 on the Sterling Highway. The road soon forks, the left leading to Kelly Lake, the right to Peterson Lake. There is no trailer ramp, but you can drive directly to the water's edge.

The Paddling

The paddling is leisurely and these lakes are great places to learn how to handle a boat. Explore around as you see fit. The best fishing will be where springs flow in. Keep the wind direction in mind, though. Wind will be calmest in the morning. In the afternoon, that can change. If you have a tailwind leaving the campground, remember you will have to fight a headwind to get back. And a headwind always blows harder than a tailwind.

24 Engineer Lake

Character: A small lake with a small informal campground, a public use cabin that includes a rowboat, and a hiking trail. Great for families with children.

Lake size: Engineer Lake is roughly 0.8 miles wide and 0.6 miles wide.

Boat types: Canoe, kayak, or rowboat.

Special features: Forgiving paddling, easy road access, a small campground, stocked fish, and an adjacent hiking trail. The Engineer Lake Public Use Cabin is available for rent by reservation and comes with its own rowboat.

Difficulties: Beginner. Class I, cold water, occasional wind.

Season: Late May through October. (The lakes can have incredible ice-skating some winters.)

Contact for more information: For campground information and cabin reservations, including a rowboat, do a web search for "Kenai National Wildlife Refuge Engineer Lake."

The view from the beach at Engineer Lake public use cabin: the boat that comes with the cabin rental and the peaks of the Kenai Mountains to the south.

Overview

Engineer Lake is a charmer that accommodates a wide range of outdoor interests. Accessed from the gravel Skilak Lake Road, Engineer sees less random people than many other road-accessible lakes on the Kenai. There are lovely views of the Kenai Mountains to the south from the cabin beach. You can either boat or hike to the Engineer Lake public use cabin rental, which also comes with its own rowboat.

General Access

Turn off from Skilak Lake Road. At the put-in, there is a small—roughly two to three spots—informal campground with a pit toilet, picnic bench, and fire rings. There is no trailer ramp, but the road goes directly to the water's edge. The southern end of the Seven Lakes Trail begins at the campground.

The Paddling

The paddling is leisurely, and this lake is a great place to learn how to handle a boat. Explore around as you see fit. Engineer Lake is connected by grown-in channels to Hidden Lake, and then Skilak Lake and the Kenai River, so it potentially has decent fishing. However, it is fished hard, and I have not observed so much as a minnow in there.

If heading to the Engineer Lake Cabin, it is about a 0.6-mile paddle across the lake directly from the campground put-in to the cabin. If walking to the cabin, it is about a mile walk from the campground to the cabin. The cabin is south facing, and on clear days has great views of the Kenai Mountains from the beach. The cabin is at the end of a 0.2-mile spur trail off the main Seven Lakes trail and so it feels quite private. The cabin comes with a rowboat rental, which, combined with the southern exposure, great views, ease of access, and variety of activities, makes this one of the most sought-after public use rentals on the Kenai Peninsula. Make your reservations early.

25 Hidden Lake

Character: A large lake with rocky coves, good fishing, and some islands. A large, formal campground is at the east end, and a hiking trail spur comes to shore at the west end.

Lake size: Roughly 4.5 miles long and 0.5 to 1 miles wide.

Boat types: Canoe or kayak.

Special features: Rocky coves, good fishing, and good access from large campground.

Difficulties: Beginner to intermediate. Class I, cold water, wind.

Season: Late May through October.

Contact for more information: For campground information and site reservations, do a web search for "Kenai National Wildlife Refuge Hidden Lake Campground."

Hidden Lake is probably called Hidden Lake because it is set low among surrounding hills.

Overview

Hidden Lake is a large lake, great for an all-day explore. There are many rocky coves and cliffs above the water. Islands in the middle make for more interest. And, a hiking trail comes down to the lake at the far end from the put-in. Connected to Skilak Lake and the Kenai River, fishing on Hidden Lake can be good.

The large campground at the east end of the lake makes a pleasant base for exploration. There is a ramp for launching trailered boats, and the majority of the boats on the water have motors. However, most people are out fishing and boats generally give each other space.

General Access

Turn off from Skilak Lake Road. The campground is at the end of a short spur. There is a trailer ramp for launching large boats.

The Paddling

Set out to explore the miles of shore. There are rocky cliffs with eagles' nests, good fishing, and islands. Make the trip your own and see what is out there. It is important, however, to keep wind direction and strength in mind. A quick paddle heading out with a tailwind makes for a tough slog on the return. Also keep in mind that on warm days, wind tends to increase in strength though the afternoon. You head in the morning in the calm, only to have the wind pick up later and make a return paddle unexpectedly difficult. Hidden Lake is a wide, cold lake, so generally stick close to shore for safety.

26 Swan Lake Canoe Route

Character: A chain of kettle lakes and two rivers linked by portage trails in a designated wilderness area.

Distance: Varies widely, see "The Paddling" sections to follow.

Estimated paddling time: Varies widely, see "The Paddling" sections to follow.

Boat types: Canoe capable of being carried on your shoulders for up to 1 mile at a stretch.

Special features: Varied and abundant wildlife, few people, and portage trails.

Difficulties: Advanced beginner. Class I, portaging requires thoughtful planning and wind can be a problem on the largest lakes.

Season: Late May through October.

Contact for more information: For general information, do a web search for "Kenai National Wildlife Refuge Swan Lake Canoe." For detailed maps and paddling information, it is still possible to find copies of the out-of-print guidebook *The Kenai Canoe Trails*, by Daniel L. Quick, ISBN 0964780402. For information about the Captain Cook State Park and Moose River State Park, do a web search for "Alaska State Parks," then for the specific name of the park.

Overview

This system of lakes and rivers connected by portage trails is larger, much emptier, and infinitely wilder than the more famous Boundary Waters in Minnesota that inspired its creation.

The possibilities for routes are almost endless. Even camping on the first lakes by the entrances can be lovely. As you travel farther into the system, the fishing just gets better and the animals more surprised by your presence. Loons may swim along in the clear water beneath your canoe while you paddle. Every lake has abundant life, from muskrats and beavers to shoreside wolves. Moose and black bears routinely appear. Trumpeter swans, exotic waterfowl, and numerous other bird species swim the shores.

And the rainbow trout fishing, although it is generally for pan fish, is like it used to be way back in the imaginary time when the fishing was always good.

This collection of glacial kettle lakes sits on fertile rolling, forested country. When the trees turn color in the short fall, the area is sublime.

There are two major reasons these routes are less popular than they deserve to be.

One is bugs. The entire area is a swamp. In June, July, and sometimes into August, the mosquitoes are something else. Try to camp on breezy points, islands, or other locations open to the wind to reduce the bugs. And bring head nets, a sealed tent in good condition, clothes mosquitoes can't bite through, and bug dope.

Two, many people who are experienced paddlers have never routinely portaged boats before and ruin their trip with improper packing. Alternately paddling then walking with a boat on your shoulders is a very different way of traveling than just paddling. It is not more difficult, but it does require thought for the special circumstances. First off, this is a formally designated wilderness area, and wheeled carts for boats are forbidden. Choose a canoe light enough that one person can carry it on

Think of the portages as fun!

their shoulders. This means the boat must either be quite small, or made from fiberglass or Kevlar, and not longer than around 16 feet regardless of the material. A padded carrying yoke helps. Then, pack your gear so it can be carried in one trip. With two people, one can carry the boat and the other the pack and paddles. The boat mule can also carry a pack of light but bulky gear, such as sleeping bags and pads, so long as the design of the pack doesn't interfere with carrying the boat. Experiment with your setup before leaving for the trip.

With this arrangement, you only have to walk the portage trail once. If another shuttle trip is necessary, it triples the total walking distance between lakes. Carrying a boat with two people is not only incredibly awkward but also requires more trips back and forth. Do not succumb to temptation and drag your boat over the trail; such mistreatment will destroy it.

Any discussion of the Swanson River and Swan Lake canoe routes is incomplete without a mention of Daniel L. Quick's classic guidebook *The Kenai Canoe Trails*. From campsite locations, to comprehensive maps overlaying aerial photographs, to fishing data, it is the most thorough and accurate source of information about this area. It even makes fun reading. Everyone canoeing on this system should have a copy.

As a final note, there are numerous established campsites throughout the system. There is no need to create your own. If all else fails, and you can't find a spot on a lake where you feel you absolutely must camp, the heads of the portage trails are usually wide enough for at least one tent, and some of them are much larger. And as the corollary to that point, most paddlers on these routes seek isolation. If you have a specific camp spot as your goal and arrive only to find it taken, move on and find a different spot well away from them. It is not hard to do in this large, wild series of canoe trails.

General Access

For all accesses: At Sterling Highway, mile 83.4, turn north onto the Swanson River Road. (There is a reliable sign indicating the turnoff.) The road soon turns to gravel. Watch for speeding oilfield workers. Dolly Varden Lake Campground is at mile 14.

Head straight (the right arm of the Y) at the oilfield road a half mile after the campground. Rainbow Lake Campground, with three campsites, is at mile 15.4. Take the right onto Swan Lake Road at mile 17 for the canoe trails; take the left to go the Swanson River.

On Swan Lake Road, drive 3 miles to the small Fish Lake Campground. The trailhead to the west entrance of the Swan Lake Canoe Route is at mile 3.5. This is by far the most popular starting point for a Swan Lake trip. The east entrance is at mile 9.5, and there is a much smaller parking area. (The first few lakes from the east entrance do not have fish in them.) Finally, Swan Lake Road dead-ends at mile 12. A short, steep walk from the parking lot leads to Paddle Lake, the first lake of the Swanson River Canoe Route.

Although these lakes are only 25 miles or so from Anchorage the way the crow flies, allow for roughly 3 hours driving time from that city to the trailhead.

The Paddling

Swan Lake Canoe Route
There are infinite possibilities for trips on the Swan Lake Route. If you are a first-time visitor, plan less ambitious trips to get acclimated—a weekend at Canoe Lake or Water Fowl Lake is a tremendous introduction to this wonderful chain of lakes.

From the West Entrance
Canoe Lake is the first lake by the entrance and is the most popular. Spruce Lake, however, is by far the most popular destination lake on this route. Spruce is large, with many established camping spots, and is around 3 hours of steady paddling and single-trip portaging into the system. It is most popular on Memorial Day weekend (when the bugs sometimes aren't that bad yet). One further portage to Trout Lake, or two to Gavia Lake, will bring more peaceful camping and better fishing.

Very few people follow the west chain of lakes from Otter to Camp Island. There is no decent fishing or campsites until the terminus at Camp Island Lake, and the only good campsite is on the island. Allow a day and a half of hard work to get there

Swan Lake Canoe Route

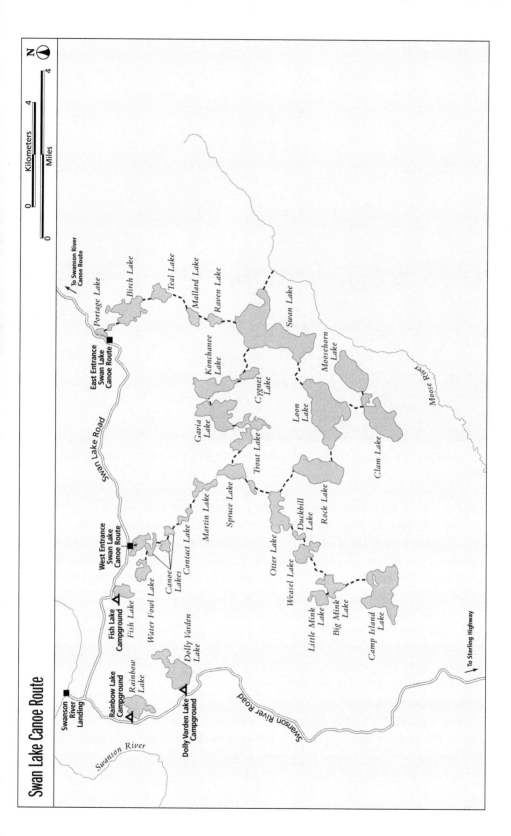

When the fishing is good, it is really, really good. This stringer of pan fish took as many casts as there are fish.

from the entrance. However, Camp Island is connected to the Moose River, and thus the Kenai River. It has huge fish and you can hook into boat-towing monsters. Some older maps show a paddle route from Camp Island to the Moose River. Do not take this unless you are prepared for a minor ordeal. Camp Island is also on the southern boundary of the wilderness area and is sometimes floated by people coming in most of the way with motors.

Heading east from Otter Lake, you encounter the big lakes of the system: Rock, Loon, and Swan, ranging from 1 to 2 miles in length. These lakes have good fishing and plentiful campsites. Allow 2 to 3 days to head out and back from the West Entrance, or to loop around to the East Entrance. A side trip to Clam and Moosehorn lakes will be rewarded with more isolation.

From the East Entrance

There are essentially no fish in the lakes from the East Entrance until Swan Lake. Hence, this chain of lakes is lightly traveled, with the few established campsites along the way used mostly by moose hunters in the fall and paddlers making a beeline for Swan Lake or the Moose River.

A half-mile portage trail leads from Swan Lake to the Moose River, the largest tributary of the fish-rich Kenai. Allow 3 to 4 days from the entrance to the takeout on the Moose River at the Izaak Walton State Recreation Site in Sterling, mile 81.9 on the Sterling Highway. Most of the Moose River is sluggish and passes beneath view-restricting bluffs. Expect to paddle steadily. Expect to encounter trees lying across the channel. The fishing and hunting along the river can be excellent, especially between the Swan Lake portage and the West Fork of the Moose River's mouth, where boats with motors are prohibited. The best camping spots on the Moose River are just above the East Fork mouth and at the West Fork mouth.

27 Swanson River Canoe Route

A short, steep portage path leads down from the parking lot to the shore of Paddle Lake, the first lake on the Swanson River Canoe Route. There are a number of excellent camping spots even on this lake. Many paddlers make the 0.5-mile first portage on to Lure Lake, and over the short portages—including over one beaver dam—to Lonely Lake. There are a number of private camping spots on these lakes and the smaller lakes between them.

Despite its name, Lonely Lake is perhaps the most popular of these lakes since it sits at the hub of a number of possible canoe trails and is about 3 hours in from the entrance. The fishing can be good here, although the fish get easily spooked when they hear a canoe in the water, especially when a paddle knocks against the side. Camping at Lonely Lake and making a day trip as far south as Mouse Lake is one of the best ways that I know of to spend a day.

A longer trip from Paddle Lake to Gene Lake will take a very full, tiring day. It is more fun to do it in 2 days. Most people follow the east chain of lakes to reach Gene since the 0.75-mile portage between Woods and Gene Lakes is shorter than the 1-mile portage between Swanson and Gene. The west chain of lakes is also worth traveling, especially if they are your final destination—Campers and Swanson Lakes have excellent fishing and pleasant campsites.

On Gene Lake, paddle through the tulies at the west end of the lake to reach a campsite on a small island. Most campers at Gene Lake seek solitude. It is the hub of a number of further routes.

The portage between Gene and Pepper Lakes is a narrow, winding channel that is fun to paddle (the Fish and Wildlife Service map incorrectly shows a hiking trail) and ends in a beaver dam you haul over to reach Pepper Lake. There is only one campsite on Pepper Lake. An excellent day can be spent exploring Twig and Birch Tree Lakes, but double back to camp at night and avoid the grown-in channel to Lynx Lake and what was once described to me as the "difficult passage" between Nuthatch and Wonder Lakes. I have never done that route since being warned—"difficult passage" is an understatement.

The eastern string of lakes from Gene Lake—Eider, Olsjold, and Wonder—are almost never traveled since they have poor fishing. The portage trail between Gene and Eider is growing in, and the sign marking the trail is not always posted. Eider and Wonder Lakes have campsites on small islands, and you can paddle between the three lakes.

The western outlet of Gene Lake flows into the Swanson River. Allow 2 to 4 days from Paddle Lake to Swanson River Landing, adding 1 or 2 days if you float the Swanson River all the way to the mouth at Captain Cook State Park. Another "difficult passage" is between Gene Lake and Swanson River, a tough 1.5 miles. You will be dragging your boat through damp ground, over beaver dams, and between grabby

Gene Lake at sunset.

Swanson River Canoe Route

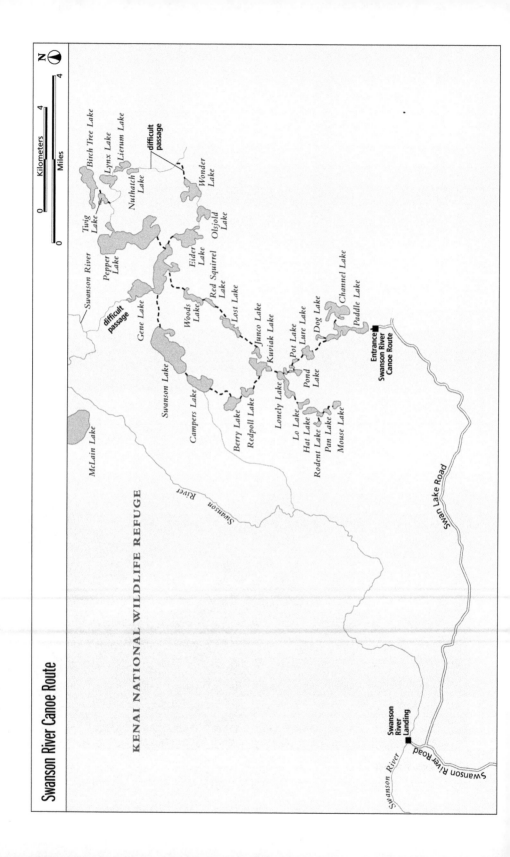

KENAI NATIONAL WILDLIFE REFUGE

McLain Lake

Swanson River

Swanson River

Birch Tree Lake

Lynx Lake

Lierum Lake

Nuthatch Lake

Twig Lake

Pepper Lake

Gene Lake

Eider Lake

Red Squirrel Lake

Olsjold Lake

Wonder Lake

difficult passage

difficult passage

Swanson Lake

Woods Lake

Lost Lake

Junco Lake

Kuviak Lake

Campers Lake

Berry Lake

Redpoll Lake

Lonely Lake

Pot Lake

Lure Lake

Dog Lake

Channel Lake

Paddle Lake

Lo Lake

Hat Lake

Pond Lake

Rodent Lake

Pan Lake

Mouse Lake

Entrance
Swanson River
Canoe Route

Swanson River

Swan Lake Road

Swanson River Landing

Swanson River Road

Swanson River Road

Kilometers
0   4

Miles
0   4

N

branches. Expect to get wet, sweaty, muddy, and bug bitten. You might even swear a bit. You can resume actual floating once the Gene Lake outlet joins the Swanson River, although there are random, boat-bashing granite boulders in the Swanson. The fiberglass boat that is so nice on the portage trails becomes a potential liability when hitting the rocks. And, once reaching the Swanson, boats with motors up to 10 horsepower are allowed, but are rarely encountered because of the rocks.

The Kenai National Wildlife Refuge operates a public use cabin on McLain Lake (N60 51.532' / W150 34.072'), a short, marked footpath from the Swanson River. Make reservations before staying there.

Takeout at Swanson River Landing, or continue on to Captain Cook State Park.

28 Kasilof River

Character: A Class II glacier-fed river with fantastic fishing.

Distance: 17 river miles total—9 miles from the Tustumena Lake Campground to the Kasilof River State Recreation Site by the Sterling Highway bridge, and a further 8 miles from there to the mouth.

Estimated paddling time: 2 hours in a kayak, 3.5 to 4 hours in a cataraft from Tustumena Lake Campground to the Kasilof River State Recreation Site, and 4 to 6 hours from there to the mouth, depending on tides.

Boat types: Drift boat, river kayak, or cataraft.

Special features: Glacial outflow and strong tides near mouth.

Difficulties: Advanced beginner. Class II, submerged rocks, cold water, tides.

Season: May through end of September.

Contact for more information: For fishing information, do a web search for "Alaska Department of Fish and Game Kasilof." For Tustumena Lake Campground information, do a web search for "Kenai National Wildlife Refuge Tustumena Campground." For Kasilof River State Recreation Sites information, do a web search for "Alaska State Parks Kasilof."

Overview

The Kasilof River is the second largest freshwater fishery on the Kenai Peninsula. Second only to the Kenai River, the Kasilof is a longer drive from Anchorage and has fewer access points from paved roads. Therefore, this stretch of water gets substantially less boat traffic than the Kenai. This is fine.

The Kasilof from the Tustumena Lake Campground to the Kasilof River State Recreation Site by the Sterling Highway bridge gets very little boat pressure and is a fun float because of it. Fishing for salmon, rainbow trout, and Dolly Varden can be outstanding. The Class II water is a fun, not overwhelming, challenge (although the water is too difficult for most canoes). Birdwatching and other wildlife-viewing opportunities are abundant; cormorants, eagles, and assorted terns are especially dense on the upper river. Brown bears and moose can stroll the banks. There are few homes along the banks.

From the Sterling Highway bridge to the mouth, it is a very different story. Guided drift boats dominate. There are substantially fewer rocks or gravel shallows in the channel. However, the only public pull-out is along the beach at the mouth—and there is no formal access there. Instead, you must make arrangements and pay for boat pull-outs with private owners. There are also many buildings and fishermen along the banks.

As a last note, the Alaska Department of Fish and Game begins their mile count on the Kasilof River from the perspective of a returning salmon. So, the mouth is mile 0, counting up against the current. Since this river is so heavily fished, this guide follows the ADF&G mile count.

Drift boats are far and away the most common boat type on the Kasilof River. Guides like them since they are stable and can tolerate repeated contact with rocks. But sometimes you have to mix things up a little and run a kayak down from the Sterling Highway bridge.

General Access

River mile 17, Tustumena Lake Campground (a.k.a. the Slackwater Boat Launch): At the end of Tustumena Lake Road. (At Sterling Highway, mile 110.3, turn onto Johnson Lake Loop Road. Take a left at the large metal T. This is Tustumena Lake Road and it frequently does not have any other road sign. Drive 6.5 miles to the end of this gravel road.) There is a boat launch, day parking, and a campground. All have nominal fees. The boat launch and day parking are operated by the Kenai National Wildlife Refuge, the campground is operated by the Cook Inlet Native Corporation (CIRI).

River mile 8, Kasilof River State Recreation Site: At Sterling Highway mile 109.4 on the east side of the road. The turnoff is clearly signed. Operated by Alaska State Parks, this well-maintained boat launch and day use area is by far the most popular put-in point on the river. Most fishing guides will meet their clients here. The standard Alaska State Parks fees apply.

River mile 7, Crooked Creek State Recreation Site: From mile 111 on the Sterling Highway turn north on Cohoe Loop Road. Drive 1.8 miles, then turn right on Rilinda Road. The entire route is well signed. This Alaska State park has day use parking and camping. It has outstanding bank fishing by the mouth of the clear-flowing Crooked Creek and is used almost entirely by bank fisherman. The only access to the river is down the steep bank on a footpath. This put-in/takeout is only suitable for boats capable of being carried by a person uphill and should only be used by kayaks. But, hey, you only have to pay for the parking.

River mile 5, Cohoe Cove Campground and RV Park: Drive 2.1 miles down Cohoe Loop Road and turn right on Webb-Ramsel Road. There is a fee boat launch here, as well as campsites catering to RVs.

River mile 1.5, Kasilof River Lodge: A private takeout within the tidal mouth of the river.

River mile 0: There is public access to the beach sands at the end of Cohoe Loop Road. Knobby tires, four-wheel drive, and high clearance are usually necessary to negotiate the soft sand. Beware of dramatic tidal surges when parking. This beach can get very crowded during personal use fisheries.

The Paddling

The 9 miles from Tustumena Lake Campground to the Sterling Highway bridge put-in pass by quickly in a plastic kayak or cataraft. This section should take roughly 3 hours, more or less, of steady paddling. The water is slack for roughly 1 mile to 1.5 miles below the campground, but quickly picks up speed.

There are two rapids shown on the map. These are Class II at most water levels and Class III at high water. They are easily negotiated in catarafts or kayaks by intermediate paddlers who are paying attention.

Be aware of frequent submerged rocks throughout the flow, though. To spot the rocks, watch for a change in water color from green to brown.

These rocks and occasional shallows in low water keep most powered boats and guides in drift boats from traveling this stretch. It is common to see no one else, although traffic is frequent enough to keep sweepers cut from the banks.

The banks are largely empty of homes until the last few bends before the bridge. Above these homes, wildlife viewing and fishing can be excellent. There are numerous rocky bends for setting up camp.

The water is green from glacial outflow and is incredibly cold. Do not flip your boat. This river does not forgive many mistakes. At high water levels, the river can get pushy and fast, demanding a stronger and more skillful paddler. Stop and look at the river at the Sterling Highway bridge before going to the put-in to double check that floating the upper river is something you want to do.

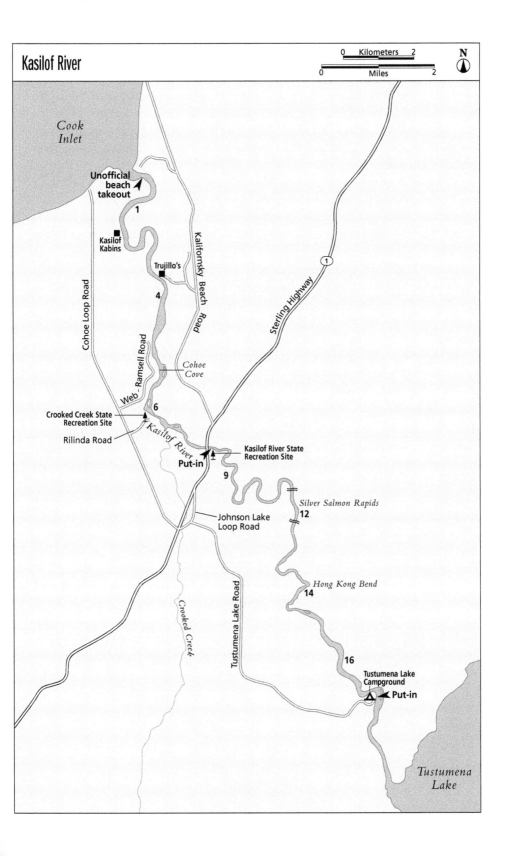

Kasilof River

0　Kilometers　2

0　Miles　2

N

Cook
Inlet

**Unofficial
beach
takeout**
1

Kasilof
Kabins

Trujillo's

4

Kalifornsky Beach Road

Sterling Highway

1

Cohoe Loop Road

Web - Ramsell Road

*Cohoe
Cove*

6

Crooked Creek State
Recreation Site

Rilinda Road

Kasilof River

Put-in

Kasilof River State
Recreation Site

9

Johnson Lake
Loop Road

Silver Salmon Rapids

12

Tustumena Lake Road

Crooked Creek

Hong Kong Bend

14

16

Tustumena Lake
Campground

Put-in

*Tustumena
Lake*

Below the Sterling Highway bridge, boat traffic picks up substantially. Fishing from motorized boats is illegal on the Kasilof, so rowed drift boats dominate the fleet. However, most drift boats do have motors for the slackwater along the tidal mouth when they are no longer fishing. Almost all boats on the water are operated by guides.

There are fewer rocks and shallows on this section compared to the upper section, but there are still riffles and rocks that require boaters to pay attention. The water is generally Class II.

The mouth of Crooked Creek on the left bank at river mile 7 will have lots of bank fishermen during salmon season. Swing wide of all fishing lines in the water.

Cohoe Cove, a private takeout, stands out clearly on the left bank at roughly river mile 5. The current slackens considerably below here and the channel is no longer so rocky.

High tide affects the river up to roughly river mile 4.5, although the emphasis is on the word "roughly." Cook Inlet has tremendous tidal differences and if you will be paddling below Cohoe Cove, wise paddlers will consult a tide chart.

Kasilof Cabins takeout is on the left bank at river mile 1.5, well within the tidal mouth.

River mile 0 is the open mouth. It can be crowded with commercial fishing boats, personal use fisheries participants, and lots of other people besides. It is not generally paddled as far as the mouth.

Northern Interior

The Northern Interior region of Alaska is protected from wet, cool weather along the coast by soaring mountain ranges. In this enormous, landlocked area, summer tends to be drier and warmer than in the rest of the state. On hot days, strong thunderstorms can develop by mid-afternoon, with powerful winds, lightning, and heavy rain. It is best to be off the water and watching the dark clouds from shore by the time they hit. The end of May through about the middle of July tends to be the warmest, driest months, with temperatures into the 70s. August through early September is usually rainy and quite cool—expect highs in the 40s and low 50s. It can snow any time of year, though.

The few roads traveling through here provide access to a surprising wealth of paddling opportunities. Fairbanks, with a population of roughly 80,000 people, is the largest city within the region, and both highways and these trips orbit around it. Fairbanks has a full range of groceries, outdoor boating stores, and transportation options, as well as cheap accommodations for the traveler willing to exert a little effort.

IV.
Northern Interior

The Northern Interior region of Alaska is protected from wet, cool weather along the coast by soaring mountain ranges. In this enormous, landlocked area, summer tends to be drier and warmer than in the rest of the state. On hot days, strong thunderstorms can develop by mid-afternoon, with powerful winds, lightning, and heavy rain. It is best to be off the water and watching the dark clouds from shore by the time they hit. The end of May through about the middle of July tends to be the warmest, driest months, with temperatures into the seventies. August through early September are usually rainy and quite cool—expect highs in the forties and low fifties. It can snow any time of year, though.

The few roads traveling through here provide access to a surprising wealth of paddling opportunities. Fairbanks, with a population of roughly 80,000 people, is the largest city within the region, and both highways and these trips orbit around it. Fairbanks has a full range of groceries, outdoor boating stores, and transportation options, as well as cheap accommodations for the traveler willing to exert a little effort.

Northern Interior

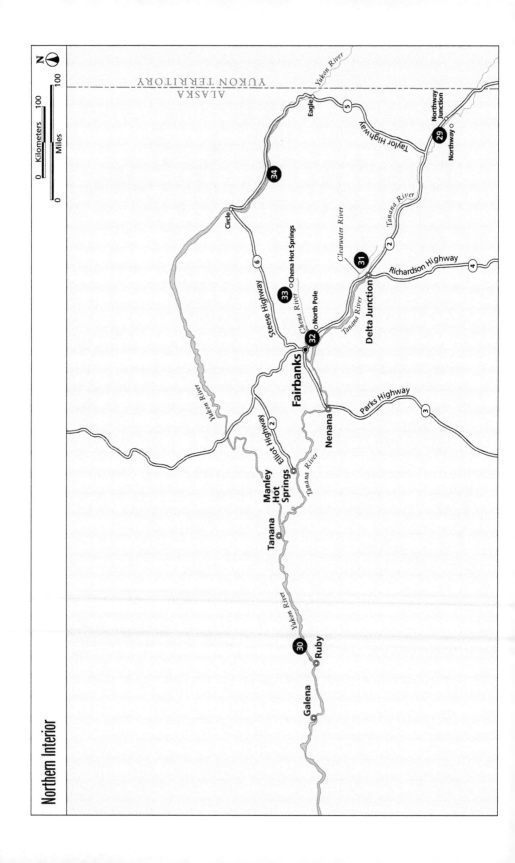

29 Upper Tanana River–Northway to George Lake Lodge

Character: A float down the upper portion of a great Interior river.
Distance: 200 miles.
Estimated paddling time: 5 to 7 days—2 to 3 days from Northway to the Alaska Highway bridge, and 3 to 4 days from the bridge to George Lake Lodge.
Boat types: Canoe, kayak, or cataraft.

Special features: Abundant bird life and great scenery.
Difficulties: Intermediate. Class I-II, choppy riffles, braided channel, wind.
Season: June through mid-September.
Contact for more information: For general area information, do a web search for "Tetlin National Wildlife Refuge."

Overview

This is perhaps one of the best places in the Interior to develop multiday paddling skills on a big river. The water is mostly flat, the braided sections are just challenging enough to be a good learning experience without causing too much anxiety, and the wind is mostly manageable.

The Upper Tanana is a long drive from Fairbanks, and is uncommonly paddled except in hunting seasons. Car shuttles present a particular difficulty since the best places to leave a vehicle for multiple nights are at Northway and George Lake Lodge, a long distance. It is much easier to arrange shorter trips if you know people in Tok or Tanacross and can leave vehicles with them, or can make arrangements to get picked up.

General Access

Northway junction: Put-in at the Chisana River. From Alaska Highway mile 1,264, turn onto Northway Road. The put-in is on the south side of the river, 0.8 miles from the Alaska Highway. If you will be leaving your vehicle unattended for days, it helps to know people in town to make arrangements for parking.

Alaska Highway bridge: Put-in/takeout at the Tanana River bridge, mile 1,304 on the Alaska Highway. The takeout is on the left bank, downstream side of the bridge. This location is suitable for drop-offs and pickups, but you will probably not want to leave a vehicle unattended for days.

Village of Tanacross: Put-in/takeout at the unmarked public landing in this small community of 144 down a short spur road from mile 1,325.7 on the Alaska Highway. There are no visitor services here. You have to know people in town to arrange parking.

George Lake Lodge: Takeout. There actually is not a lodge here at mile 1,385 on the Alaska Highway, but there used to be, and USGS maps name the location. There is only an access road to the Tanana and parking.

The mountains hover over the dramatic approach to Cathedral Rapids. The rapids themselves are more of a riffle.

The Paddling

Miles 0 to 4: Float down the small, winding Chisana River until the Nabesna River joins the flow. Now the water is officially the Tanana River.

Miles 4 to 61: The Tanana is a slow, muddy river through fertile swamps. It can be difficult to find firm camp spots, but try to land on the most upstream point of an island or mud bar for the most solid ground. The Teslin River joins the flow at river mile 50. The Alaska Highway bridge is at mile 61.

Miles 61 to 115: The river is now wider and faster in places. There is no public access between the bridge and Tanacross, but there are a few homes and camps along the river. The ground is a little firmer for camping, especially around the sections of high, rocky bluffs.

Upper Tanana River—Northway to George Lake Lodge

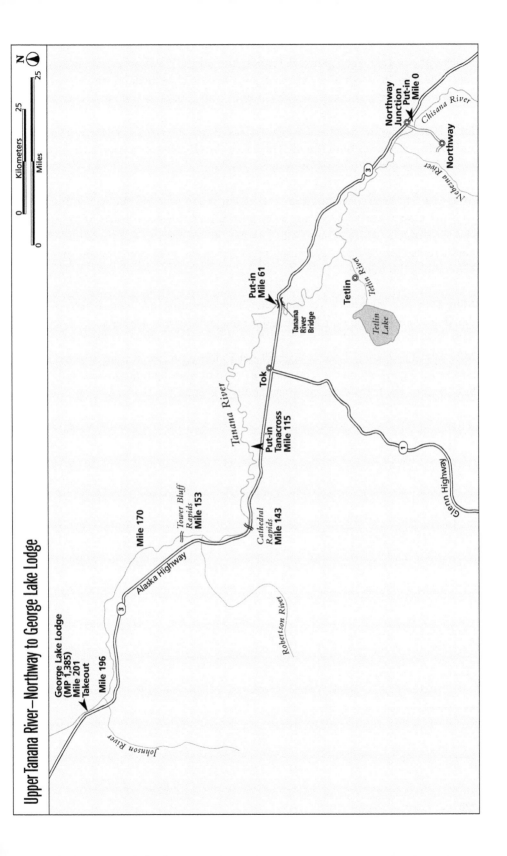

Miles 115 to 153: The Cathedral Rapids, marked on USGS maps, are more of a riffle. There are no rocks in the channel, just a few small to medium standing waves. USGS maps show a road here, as well as some camps, but there is no public access.

Mile 153: Below the mouth of the Robertson River, the channel becomes braided and is called the Tower Bluff Rapids. These Class I to II riffles are a good introduction to paddling braided water and last roughly 3 miles.

Mile 170: The river splits into many fine channels. Try to follow the widest channel with the most water while staying away from spruce tree–lined banks. If forced to choose between a channel lined with poplars and one with spruce trees, follow the poplar route. Spruce trees have strong roots and make more sweepers and strainers than other kinds of trees.

Mile 196: The Johnson River joins the Tanana, creating still more braids. Begin thinking about following the left bank since the pull-out is in 5 miles.

Mile 201: The George Lake Lodge pull-out is difficult to see; it is just a gravel gap between the greenery on the left shore. The current is strong through here, so try to line up along the left well before reaching the pull-out.

30   Tanana River to Yukon River–Fairbanks to Galena

Character: A long paddle through bush Alaska along wide, wide rivers.

Distance: Fairbanks to Nenana is 52 miles, Nenana to Manley Hot Springs is 107 miles, and Fairbanks to Galena is 400 miles.

Estimated paddling time: Fairbanks to Nenana is roughly 2 days, Nenana to Manley Hot Springs is 4 to 5 days, and Fairbanks to Galena is between 2 and 3 weeks, depending on wind and water levels.

Boat types: Canoe, with a keel, or sea kayak.

Special features: Bush Alaska and wide river.

Difficulties: Intermediate. Class I, wind can churn the river into 10-foot waves, and you must pull over and camp to wait the weather out.

Season: Early June through mid-September.

Contact for more information: For boat and gear rentals, do a web search for "Alaska Outdoor Rental and Guides."

Overview

This journey begins in Alaska's second largest city and travels through the roadless Interior. This is the Alaska that people hear about but rarely experience for themselves. Only a few groups make this trip each year. Many residents in villages live a subsistence lifestyle. Bird densities can be incredible. There are numerous camping spots on the islands and gravel bars in the river.

Past the town of Nenana, this becomes a long paddle. The water is almost entirely Class I, so you need to develop the mentality of a long-distance hiker, but using a boat. The estimated paddling times above assume paddling 8 hours a day. Developing a routine of breaking camp every morning, eating breakfast, loading the boat, and getting on the water is important. Once underway, the current is surprisingly strong, and mileage is largely a function of time spent on the water, although you will develop strong paddling muscles from using them all day long. Quick stops for lunch, followed by more hours on the water in the afternoon are necessary. This is a trip for people who like to be in boats.

This is also a trip for people who like to camp. There are no real visitor facilities anywhere along the route. Tanana, Ruby, and Galena have washeterias—combination laundromat and showers. There are bed-and-breakfasts in the villages, but they will probably be fully booked in the summer. Once you leave the road system, you won't find signs on most businesses, so you have to ask around to locate them. You must be skilled at drying gear, washing clothes, and the other routines of living outside, all while not thinking of the temptation of sleeping under a roof.

The town of Nenana and the village of Tanana have grocery stores suitable for restocking a week or so worth of food, but the more food you can bring from the beginning of the trip, the easier it will be.

Always bring days more food than necessary. These are big rivers and the wind blows hard. Boat-swamping waves can be common in some spots, and camping for days on shore while waiting out the weather will almost certainly happen at least once or twice on this trip.

A sea kayak paddles much faster on this water than a canoe because of the kayak's ability to slice through winds and waves. However, kayakers will find their boat confining to sit in all day long, as well as on the small side for storage capacity. You will have to stop to restock food at least once or maybe twice.

A canoe is comfortable to paddle all day long because it is easy to shift body positions throughout the day. Canoes can also carry enough food for the entire trip, making restocking voluntary. However, canoes are much harder to paddle into a headwind and cannot handle big waves as well as a kayak. Plan on taking more weather days in a canoe than in a kayak.

If flying out of Galena, boat size is not a problem since they are loaded into large, empty cargo planes. There is no need to have a folding boat. If you feel you must leave from the smaller villages of Tanana or Ruby, then you will need a folding boat to get on a small mail plane.

The forested, rolling hills above these broad valleys make this a lovely trip to do in the fall, as the leaves are turning. Setting out in early September, you should hit the peak of the color. However, winds are stronger in the fall, and you will probably have to paddle late at night to find calm water. Also, be prepared for the first freezes and snows of the year in the month of changing seasons.

General Access

Put-in: Chena Pump Road Public Access. There is an improved boat ramp for direct access to the Tanana.

Takeouts:
Nenana: Land at the public beach on the left, just before the Parks Highway bridge. This is not a good place to leave gear unattended for long periods of time.

Manley Hot Springs: It is a couple miles walk from the beach on the Tanana to the town of Manley Hot Springs. Turn up the slough and paddle hard if you want to get there directly. It is easiest to just not stop here if you are on a through-paddle.

Galena: Land at the broad public beach on the right. Fly back to Fairbanks from here, loading your boat and cargo onto regularly scheduled passenger and/or cargo flights.

The Paddling

Chena Pump Road put-in, mile 0: Standing on the beach, you get the sensation of just how wide a river the Tanana is.

Tanana River to Yukon River—Fairbanks to Galena

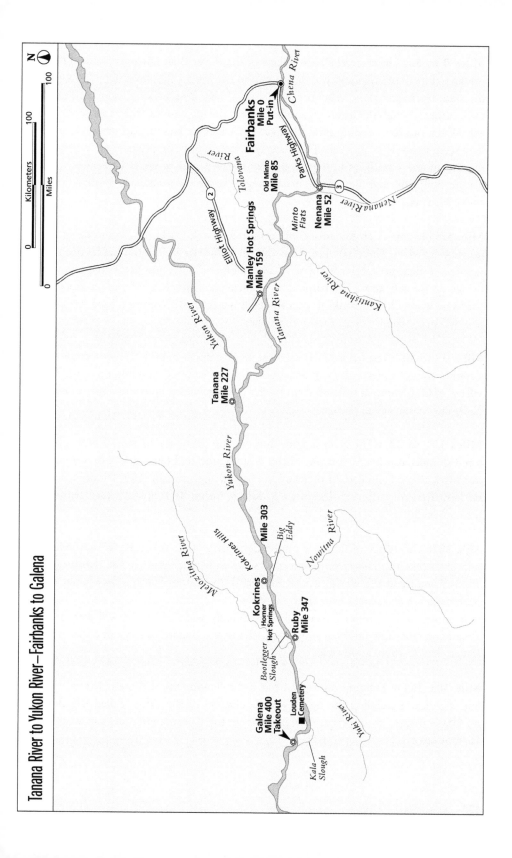

Miles 0 to 52: The recreated bush village of the River Boat Discovery tours line is on the left bank point as you paddle away from the put-in. Homes will be visible on the right bluffs, and if the wind is calm, you will hear dogs barking, vehicles, and so on. Cutting through the inside channels shortens the big bends of the river considerably. Watch out for speeding skiffs, though. For whatever reason, skiff drivers around here seem unaware of paddlers. There are numerous camps on points used mostly by moose hunters. Check for no trespassing signs before landing since there are a lot of private camps through here. The current begins to slow considerably about 5 miles above Nenana.

Mile 52: Nenana. A grounded steamer on the left bank marks the beginning of this inland port town. There are numerous informal landings before the public beach, a number of them private. Read the signs. The public landing is just before the highway bridge on the left, above the barge dock. Nenana has motels, a cafe, and a grocery/hardware store. The Fairbanks to Nenana float is a relatively common long weekend trip, and many paddlers end their journey here.

Miles 53 to 107: The Minto Flats can host massive flocks of birds. The current is also sluggish, and 20-miles-a-day can be a good day in a canoe, depending on wind. The village of Old Minto at mile 85 is no longer a village and is now a treatment center. They discourage casual visitors.

Miles 107 to 227: The river is wide, but cutting off bends by taking more sheltered sloughs also keeps you out of the wind. Large fuel tanks and a gravel landing mark the 2.5-mile road to Manley Hot Springs at mile 159. Paddle a little farther, then turn up the slough to paddle to town. It is an awkward stop for through-paddlers.

Mile 227: The village of Tanana is on the right bank of the Yukon River on the high side of the mouth. The river junction is wide, wide, wide and can be dangerously windy. Landing at the beach, it is a short walk to the riverside grocery store. The washeteria is a few blocks back from the river.

From now on, the Yukon River will be extremely wide and wind will present an almost constant difficulty. Plan your zigzags across the channel to stay out of the wind and as close to shore as possible.

Mile 303: Begin hugging the right bank and following the sheltered channels that hug it to avoid paddling through the wide channel of Big Eddy (called Big Bend on USGS maps). Strong winds flow down from the Kokrine Hills and can whip up 10-foot waves.

Mile 347: The village of Ruby climbs the left bank up from the river. Follow Bootlegger Slough above town, then cross the river to the village to mostly avoid the large waves along the bluffs on river-left above town. This community of several hundred people has few visitor facilities. A 50-mile gravel road leads to gold mines in the hills south of town.

Mile 400: Galena! Land at the broad public beach. A store and the washeteria are a block back from the bank. The town parallels the runway and river. The airport is accessed from the west end of the runway. A large grocery store is on the road east of the beach. If you will be spending a few days in Galena, camp on the banks before reaching the beach. Walk in from the river to the road, and mark your spot. Many people will give you rides if you are walking around town.

31　Clearwater River to Clearwater Lake

Character: A lovely early- and late-season float with clear water and a short against-the-current paddle to the lake.
Distance: 11 miles.
Estimated paddling time: 5 to 7 hours.
Boat types: Kayak or catatraft with a small motor (canoes are marginal). There is a 1-mile paddle against the current at the end of the trip, making a kayak by far the most suitable boat.
Special features: An early season, clearwater paddle with fantastic fishing. An almost com-plete loop. A short paddle against the current. Combination river and lake paddle.
Difficulties: Intermediate. Class I to II, riffles. It can get very windy. Must be a strong paddler to go against the current. Motorboat traffic can be hazardous on this narrow body of water.
Season: Late April through October, although during the height of the fishing season motorboat traffic makes the river unsafe and unpleasant for paddlers.
Contact for more information: For camp-ground information, do a web search for "Alaska State Parks Clearwater."

Overview

The Clearwater River is one of the first floats possible in the Interior spring. Around late April and early May, there are few motorboats on the river, and this route is almost (but not quite) taken over by paddlers.

There is quite a variety of water for such a short paddle. The Clearwater River itself is Class I to II riffles and a pleasant float. Second homes and camps line the upper two-thirds of the river, and the campground at the put-in can be a loud, popular spot. But what really distinguishes this trip are the numerous fish sitting at the bot-tom of most holes in the spring—sight fishing the multitude can be fantastic. And the opportunity to do a short, against-the-current paddle from the Tanana River up to Clearwater Lake makes this a rare opportunity to make an almost complete loop paddle trip.

General Access

It is possible to do this trip in 1 day based from Fairbanks, but it will be a 14-hour-plus day including driving. A more pleasant alternative is to make it an overnight.

To park the shuttle vehicle at the takeout, go straight on Triple H Road, even after it changes from pavement to graded dirt at the yield sign at Olmstead Road. Follow the landing sign to the gravel parking area by Clearwater Lake. There are some homes on the lake, so it is not isolated.

The put-in at Clearwater State Recreation Area (also called, confusingly, the Delta-Clearwater Campground on one road sign) is a utilitarian place to sleep, but not the most tranquil spot: the sixteen camping spaces are next to the road, and there is an intermittently open bar directly at the exit. There are fees for camping

This sign marks the turn for the uphill paddle to Clearwater Lake.

and parking in season. There is a concrete boat ramp here as well, since motorboats frequently travel the river, especially during the height of salmon season.

As a further note, this trip is ideal for using a bike as a shuttle vehicle, making only one gas-consuming car necessary. Lock your bike in the trees at Clearwater Lake, then pedal the flat 8.5 miles back to the campground to pick up the vehicle. The shoulder is wide and traffic is light with plenty of sight warning on the approach. The wind can blow hard in Delta, which can make the entire ride seem uphill, but it should take a little less than 1 hour to bike back.

The Paddling

Put-in at Clearwater State Recreation Area Campground to the Tanana River: The Clearwater River is a relatively narrow channel with tight bends. There are few sweepers and snags since motorboat operators tend to clear the channel. Except for the odd riffle, it is mostly moving Class I flatwater. There are frequent deep pools. Second homes and camps dot the shore in every logical place to stop until the first stringer of the Tanana River enters the Clearwater. (The Tanana is heavily silted, and the water will turn from clear to milky at this point.) The only decent camping spots (and there are only a few) begin once the Tanana joins the Clearwater. This is below the best fishing.

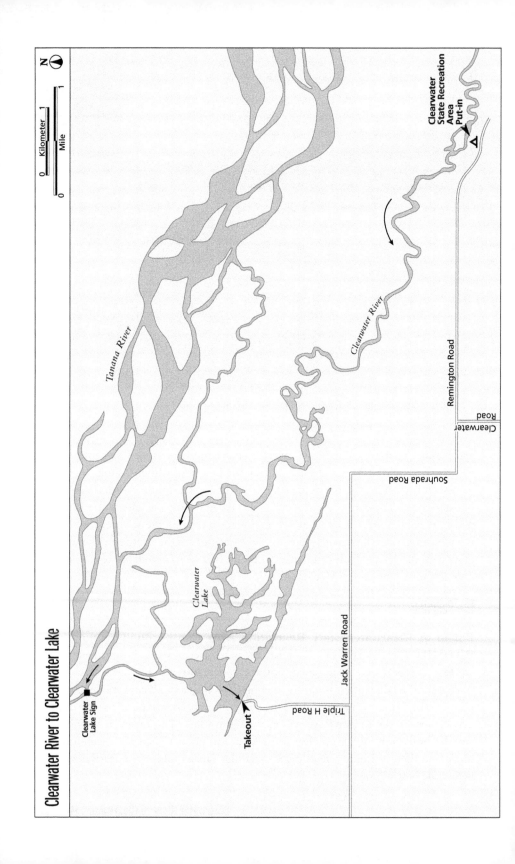

Clearwater River to Clearwater Lake

Once reaching the mainstem Tanana (after the water turns completely milky), hold tightly to the left bank. There should be a clear sign pointing to the turnoff to Clearwater Lake (approximately N64 10562' / W145 60226'), although, like anything else, there is no guarantee it will be there—the sign is maintained informally by civic-minded paddlers.

(If you miss the turnoff to Clearwater Lake, it is a 13.5-mile paddle down the Tanana to the Richardson Highway bridge in Big Delta. The Tanana is Class I water and a wide, easily navigated channel, but it can get windy. Takeout on the left either at Rika's Roadhouse or at the boat launch by the bridge and pipeline).

The paddle up the Clearwater Lake outlet channel is just long enough to be interesting and short enough not to be an ordeal. The current is strongest at the mouth and weakens the closer you get to the lake. The banks and bottom are muddy, making it difficult to line a boat against the current. The wind can really blow in this area, and the combination of a headwind and fighting the current can make the going challenging in spots; hence the strong recommendations to only do this paddle in a kayak.

From the head of Clearwater Lake outlet, paddle straight across the lake to the takeout. There are a number of private homes on the lake.

32 Chena Lake Recreation Area

Character: A popular paddle that is fun for the whole family.
Lake size: 250 acres.
Boat types: Any, including paddleboards.
Special features: Picnic areas on island, a playground, boat rentals, a swimming area, and easy access from Fairbanks.

Difficulties: Beginner. Class I. It can get crowded on hot, sunny days.
Season: June through September.
Contact for more information: For general information, do a web search for "Fairbanks Northstar Borough Chena Lake."

Overview and the Paddling

This popular lake and Chena River put-in just outside of Fairbanks is a great place for families to play around with a boat. The conditions on the small lake are forgiving enough that it is a great place to learn to paddle. There are picnic spots on an island that older children will appreciate visiting. A boat launch, swimming area, pit toilets, campsites, and boat rental round out the facilities. Just a bit down the road is Chena River Park, with campsites and a boat ramp around the slough at the base of a Chena River flood control dam. Access fees are charged from Memorial Day through Labor Day.

General Access

Take the Chena Lakes exit at mile 346.7 on the Richardson Highway. Drive on Laurance Road for 5.5 miles, past the fee-accepting guardhouse, then turn left onto Lake Park Road.

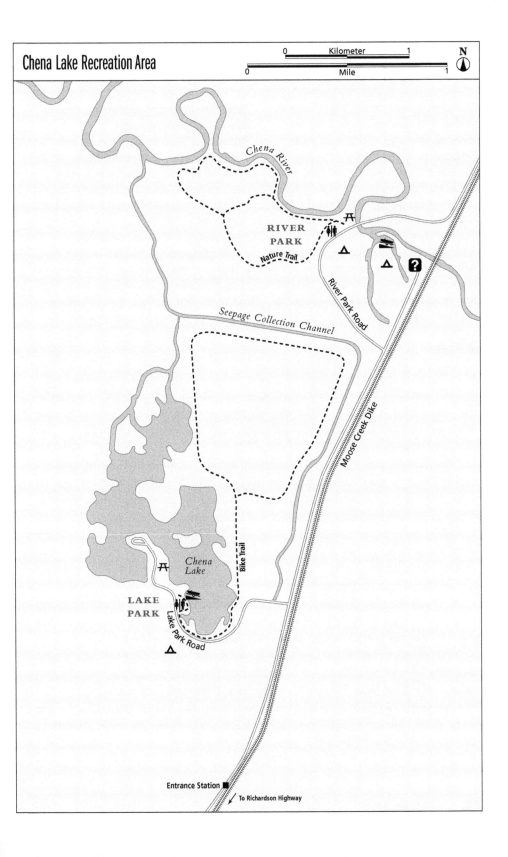

Chena Lake Recreation Area

0 Kilometer 1

0 Mile 1

N

Chena River

RIVER PARK

Nature Trail

Seepage Collection Channel

River Park Road

Moose Creek Dike

Bike Trail

Chena Lake

LAKE PARK

Lake Park Road

Entrance Station
To Richardson Highway

33 Upper Chena River–Fourth Bridge to Grange Hall Road

Character: A clearwater small river float with multiple road access points near Fairbanks.
Distance: 4th Bridge to 3rd Bridge is 7 miles. 3rd Bridge to 2nd Bridge is 6 miles. 2nd Bridge to 1st Bridge is 2.5 miles. 1st Bridge to Rosehip Campground is 17 miles. Rosehip Campground to Grange Hall Road is 12 miles.
Estimated paddling time: Alaska State Parks recommends the rule of thumb of 1 hour of float time for every 1 mile of Chena Hot Springs Road between put-in and takeout. In a kayak, you can easily halve that.
Boat types: Flat bottom canoe, river kayak, or small light cataraft.

Special features: Easy road access, clear water, and a public use cabin.
Difficulties: The skill required varies with different sections; see the descriptions in "The Paddling" section to follow. Class II, snags and sweepers, channel-blocking log jams (especially on the North Fork), low water late in summer.
Season: Mid- to late May through July.
Contact for more information: For area information including camping, do a web search for "Alaska State Parks Chena." Chena Hot Springs is a private resort at the end of the road with camping, hotels, and pools of hot water.

Overview

The Upper Chena River, defined for this guidebook as the water within the Chena River Recreation Area and down to Grange Hall Road, is one of the most popular river floats around Fairbanks. The clear-flowing water, gravel bars, and many road crossings, campgrounds, and public use cabins make this a very flexible place to plan different length floats.

The channel below the 1st Bridge is frequently ice-free by late May and is among the first floats of the year for many people. The river, however, can be more difficult to float earlier in the season because of ice damage from breakup, which uproots trees and erodes banks, creating snags and sweepers. These tend to be cleared by conscientious paddlers throughout the season, but there is no guarantee of an obstacle-free paddle.

Of course, these trips have the added attraction of a day's paddle followed by a soak in Chena Hot Springs at the end of the road.

Although there is no shoulder on Chena Hot Springs Road, there are many long straightaways with good visibility to vehicles, and a bicycle shuttle between takeout and put-in works well except on high-traffic holidays and weekends.

The put-ins and takeouts are mostly at numbered bridges, which can be a little confusing to remember. Just keep in mind that the numbers increase from the perspective of a driver from Fairbanks, not from a paddler going down the river.

Camping is allowed along the river throughout the recreation area, and there is one public use cabin, the Chena River Cabin, directly on the bank. Reserve it through Alaska State Parks.

General Access

4th Bridge: Mile 48.9, Chena Hot Springs Road, the Angel Rocks trailhead.

3rd Bridge: Mile 44, Chena Hot Springs Road.

2nd Bridge: Mile 39.5, Chena Hot Springs Road. Park either at the gravel bar on the river or by Granite Tors trailhead.

1st Bridge: Mile 37.8, Chena Hot Springs Road. Park on the unimproved gravel road on the southwest side of the bridge.

Rosehip Campground: Mile 27, Chena Hot Springs Road.

Grange Hall Road: Mile 20.8, Chena Hot Springs Road.

There are numerous informal access points to the Chena throughout this section. If you plan to takeout at one of these places, you might want to temporarily mark (and, crucially, unmark when done) the location since they are not always plain to spot from the water.

The Paddling

4th Bridge to 3rd Bridge: The North Fork of Chena River is much narrower, faster, and filled with more woody debris than the lower river. *This section is only suitable for experienced whitewater paddlers.* Water levels are generally too low to float later in summer. Expect many sweepers and strainers, as well as channel-blocking jams. Expect to portage or line the boat around obstacles. It is also best done on hot days since you will probably get wet.

3rd Bridge to 2nd Bridge: The North Fork is quickly joined by the East Fork from the left, adding more water to the flow and a wider channel. There is frequently a logjam just below the 3rd Bridge and choppy water at the East Fork confluence. *This section is also suitable only for experienced paddlers.*

2nd Bridge to 1st Bridge: This section is consistently wider and easier to float than the upriver sections. Intermediate paddlers will do fine. Still, a small, easily maneuvered boat makes the float much easier, and there are numerous sweepers and snags.

1st Bridge to Rosehip Campground: The water flows at a more sedate speed though here, but there are still riffles, snags, and sweepers. There are a number of broad gravel bars relatively far from the road, which make for nice camp or picnic

Upper Chena River – 4th Bridge to Grange Hall Road

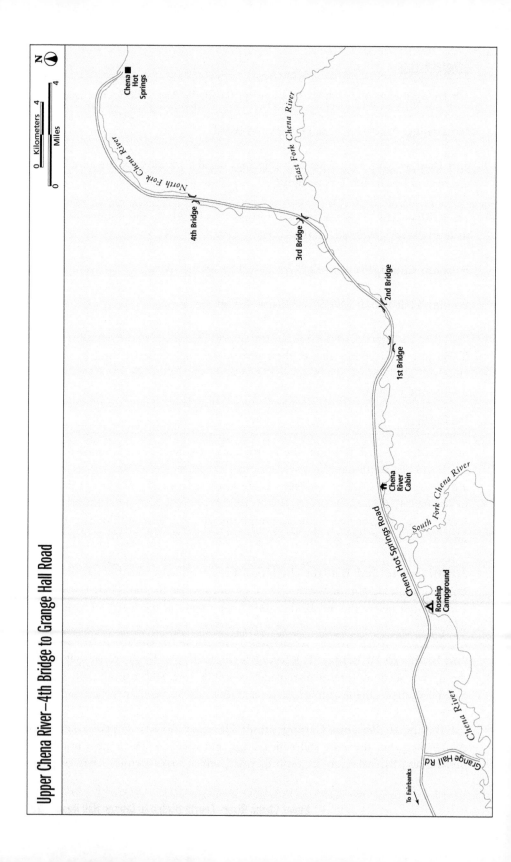

spots. The Chena River public use cabin is on river-right. There is an island, the water picks up speed, and the channel narrows as the South Fork joins the flow. The left channel around the island can be wider with more water. Keep an eye out for Rosehip Campground; it is not blindingly obvious from the water.

Rosehip Campground to Grange Hall Road: The gradient flattens below the campground and the current slows. Advanced beginners can float this section. At most water levels, there are exposed gravel banks on the bends, which make pleasant camp or picnic spots. When the channel begins to fray around 6.5 miles below the campground, choose the widest channel with the most water. The Grange Hall Road takeout is not obvious, so give it a scout on the drive to the put-in. It is a bit more than two bends after the frayed channels merge with the main flow.

34 Yukon River—Eagle to Circle

Character: A flatwater float through gold country on a legendary river.
Distance: 150 miles.
Estimated trip time: 3 to 7 days.
Boat types: Canoe (preferably with a keel), or sea or river kayak.
Special features: Public use cabins, side hiking trails, and lovely bluffs.

Difficulties: Intermediate. Class I, wind, current.
Season: Early June to late September.
Contact for more information: For area information, do a web search for "Yukon-Charley National Preserve."

Overview

This float on the upper Yukon River flows through the heart of the country where many Alaska legends were created. The town of Eagle was founded by real estate scammers during the Klondike Gold Rush, but accidentally turned out to be ideally suited as a river port to other inland gold discoveries. Roald Amundson, leaving his ship in the frozen sea ice during the first successful navigation of the Northwest Passage, journeyed by dogsled 500 miles from the Arctic Ocean to Eagle where he telegraphed news of his triumph to the world. The town of Circle, which marks the end of this float, provided river access to the first major gold strike in Alaska (predating the Klondike by a decade) and was once known as the "largest log cabin city in the world."

The river provides the modern paddler a clear, uncrowded trail through the material remains of this history. The route passes through the Yukon-Charley National Preserve, a unit of the National Park Service, and is visitor friendly. There are four, first come, first served public use cabins to get out of the rain and bugs and a number of side hikes away from the river to historic mining operations. There are also a number of old roadhouses and historic cabins to visit along the riverbank.

Autumn is an especially gorgeous time to visit the area. The combination of changing foliage and wildlife in their final burst of activity before the descending winter is spectacular.

The Yukon River is rapids- and portage-free on this stretch, but the water is not entirely without risk, and the penalties for mistakes can be severe. The current is quite swift, especially at high water in June. There is so much silt in the water that the rasping of sand grains against the boat hull will provide a constant background noise. If you capsize the boat, besides the very real danger of losing your gear, the dirt can fill your clothes, dragging even strong swimmers to the bottom.

July and August—when the water is lower, more sluggish, and a little less dirty—is a considerably more forgiving time to paddle than the June runoff peak. *Do not attempt this trip if you are an inexperienced paddler.* There are many much more forgiving places to learn. These warnings are not meant to discourage, just to caution. Pay attention and

Gravel bar camps have fewer bugs and are less likely to be visited by bears than shore camps. They are also spacious places to spread out and reorganize gear on long trips.

you should be safe, but there are a few key things to keep in mind. Get off the river quickly when the wind picks up since waves can get quite large. Hang back from the bluff bases since many weird currents boil there. And, of course, have fun.

General Access

Eagle sits at the end of the remote Taylor Highway. There is one gas station between Eagle and the Alaska Highway. Circle sits at the end of the remote Steese Highway. Shuttling boats, people, and gear between these two towns make this trip somewhat of a challenge.

Access to Eagle is a bit difficult. The two choices are to drive a private vehicle on the highway or else to arrange a chartered small plane. Circle also only has the highway and chartered small plane service.

You should arrive in Eagle with all the groceries and camping gear needed for the trip since shopping opportunities in this small community are limited.

The Paddling

Besides the formal campsites listed below, any gravel bar makes an ideal camp—the breeze over the open ground keeps the bugs down, and it can be considerably more comfortable than sleeping on shore. You are also much less likely to encounter bears or other animals on a mid-river camp.

Mile 0: The city of Eagle has a number of services: a motel, bed-and-breakfasts, and a very small grocery store. The National Park Service maintains a visitor center at the end of the airstrip.

Mile 15: Calico Bluff looms over the left bank. The alternating layers of limestone and sulfurous shale are a river landmark. Today it signals the beginning of the Yukon-Charley National Preserve. In days past, the bluffs meant you were almost in Eagle if you were traveling upriver on a steamboat.

Mile 50: Christopher "Phonograph" Nelson—nicknamed for his nonstop chatter—built the Nation Bluff Cabin (N65 20342' / W141 73822') in 1935 from the remains of an old, short-lived coal mine that once provided fuel for steamboats. There are still a few small coal piles and foundation depressions left from mining operations. The National Park Service restored the cabin for public use in 1995.

Mile 52: Nation City sits on the left bank just downriver from the mouth of the Nation River and just above the mouth of Fourth of July Creek. There are no longer any standing buildings—they have rotted away, been scavenged for logs, or been washed away by breakup ice in the spring. A few ruins remain that are two or three logs high. An old road leads 7 miles through the woods, passing an old farm a half mile

High bluffs define the channel through most of the Yukon-Charley.

from Nation, before dead-ending at an abandoned but privately owned gold mine. The path is clear and makes a nice leg-stretching stroll through the woods. However, it is important to respect the private property along the way.

On the right bank of the river, nearly opposite Nation, sits Taylor Camp. The location appears on older maps but burned to the ground in a 1999 forest fire.

James Taylor (no relation to the singer) built this homestead in stages, beginning in 1924 and continuing until he left for Seattle in 1934 with terminal cancer. He was a bit of an eccentric who built elaborate (by bush standards) log barns to house his dog team in comfort.

Mile 60: The Glen Creek public use cabin (N65 29988' / W142 0899') is plainly visible from the river on the left bank just before the Rusty Mountain bluff. Originally a hunting camp built by a Fairbanks doctor in the 1950s, it is now a nice place for paddlers to get out of the rain.

Mile 76: A large Han Native settlement existed for many centuries somewhere near the mouth of the Kandik River. The residents fished for salmon in the many swirling eddies along the Kandik mouth. The last village chief, Charley, lends his English name to a river and the preserve.

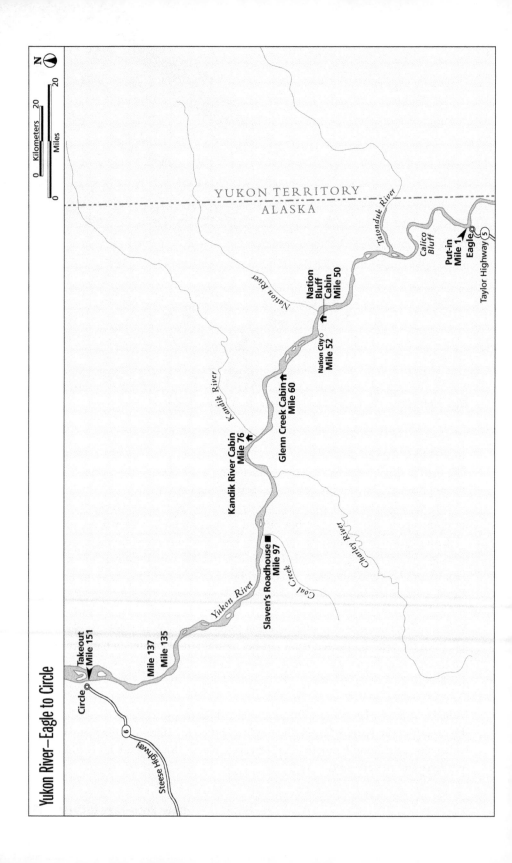

Yukon River—Eagle to Circle

N

Kilometers
0   20

Miles
0   20

YUKON TERRITORY
ALASKA

Tatonduk River

Nation River

Calico Bluff

Put-in
Mile 1
Eagle

Taylor Highway 5

Nation Bluff
Cabin
Mile 50

Nation City
Mile 52

Kandik River

Glenn Creek Cabin
Mile 60

Kandik River Cabin
Mile 76

Charley River

Slaven's Roadhouse
Mile 97

Coal Creek

Yukon River

Mile 137
Mile 135

Takeout
Mile 151

Circle

Steese Highway 6

The Kandik River public use cabin (N65 37613' / W142 51291') is just past the river mouth on the right bank, up a trail a quarter mile from the river. Larry Rickets and Jean Trainor built it in 1981 to support their subsistence lifestyle, before passing it on to the Park Service.

Beiderman's Camp sits on the left bank, slightly downriver from the mouth of the Kandik. This is private property and should be respected as such. The camp is a checkpoint for the Yukon Quest sled dog race in winter.

Mile 97: Slaven's Roadhouse sits on the left bank just below the mouth of Coal Creek. There is a visitor center and public use cabin here (N65 35054' / W143 12'). This is also a checkpoint for the Yukon Quest. A mile-long gravel road leads from the cabin to the Coal Creek Dredge, a building-sized machine that worked gold-bearing gravels until the 1960s.

Mile 135: After passing the mouth of Twenty-two Mile Creek, you leave the Yukon-Charley Preserve.

Mile 137: Fourteenmile Grave watches the Yukon flow by from its high bluff on the north bank. Its name clearly gives the distance to Circle.

Mile 151: Circle! Alas, the end of this journey. Despite a population of one hundred people through the winter, the steady road traffic allows a wide variety of services including a small grocery store, cafe, and motel. A public campground sits directly on the river where it catches the breeze to hold the bugs down.

Although it is the site of the first major gold rush in Alaska, Circle is not touristy. There will probably be a few RVs parked in the campground, but that is about it. The community is named Circle because the founding miners originally thought it sat directly on the Arctic Circle line. The town is actually a little more than 50 miles south of the point where the sun doesn't set on the summer solstice.

V.
Southern Interior

Like the Northern Interior, the Southern Interior tends to have warmer, drier summers than the rest of the state. This area, protected from the ocean by mountains, is so large that it is divided into two sections for the purposes of this book. The channels in the Southern Interior tend to be equally accessible from both Anchorage and Fairbanks and get traffic from both metropolises.

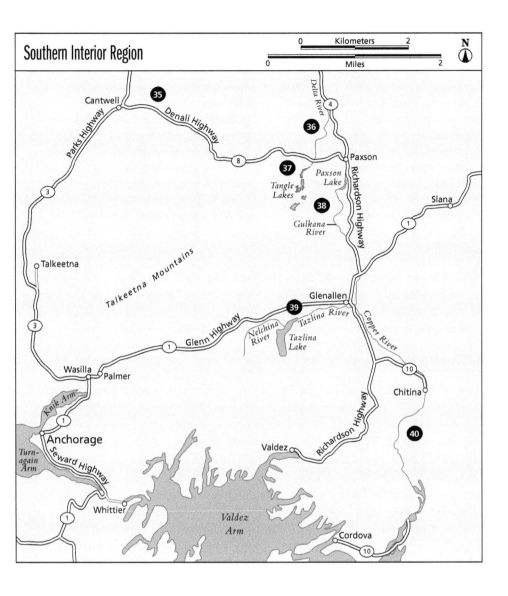

Southern Interior Region

35 Nenana River–Reindeer Hills

Character: A road-accessible float that feels quite remote. Gorgeous scenery and lots of potential camping spots.
Distance: Approximately 18 miles.
Estimated paddling time: At higher water, roughly 4 hours; at lower water, 5 to 6 hours.
Boat types: Cataraft or river kayak; the boat and paddler must be able to ferry out of the current to avoid sweepers.

Special features: Fabulous scenery and wilderness feel.
Difficulties: Intermediate. Class II, sweepers.
Season: Mid-June through mid-September.
Contact for more information: For Native corporation land ownership boundaries, do a web search for "Ahtna Land Map." The river gauge by Windy Bridge is viewable online by searching for "Alaska River Forecast Center."

Overview

This is an awesome weekend float. The Reindeer Hills and Panorama Mountain tower over the valley. Abundant gravel bars create lots of camping choices. The Class II water is straightforward enough for an experienced paddler to navigate. It is a great way to quickly get off the road, with easy put-in and takeout at roads.

General Access

Put-in: Mile 118, Denali Highway. Put in right off the road. At most water levels, you can back a trailer to the edge—but not at high water. Parking is in the lot 100 yards to the east of the put-in. It looks as if there is a put-in at mile 120 of the Denali Highway, but the ground does not slope to the water's edge nor is there any parking there.

Takeout: Beneath Windy Bridge, mile 215 of the Parks Highway. An unmarked gravel road leaves the Parks Highway about 0.4 miles southwest of the Windy Bridge. There is lots of space to back a trailer to the water and for parking.

The wide shoulder on the Parks Highway and lower traffic density on the gravel Denali Highway make this trip a good one for a bicycle shuttle. You just have to be okay with eating a little dust or mud spray on the Denali Highway while you bike.

The Paddling

Put-in off the Denalil Highway. After a few bends, you will almost touch the Denali Highway again near the mile 120 marker. After this point, the main channel of the river leaves the road and creates a hypotenuse of the triangle between it and the Denali and Parks Highways.

As you begin floating, you will observe lots of "posted" signs along shore. Ahtna, the regional Native corporation, owns most land above the high-water line through the upper half of this float and trespassing is not allowed without a permit. This is not

Upper Nenana River

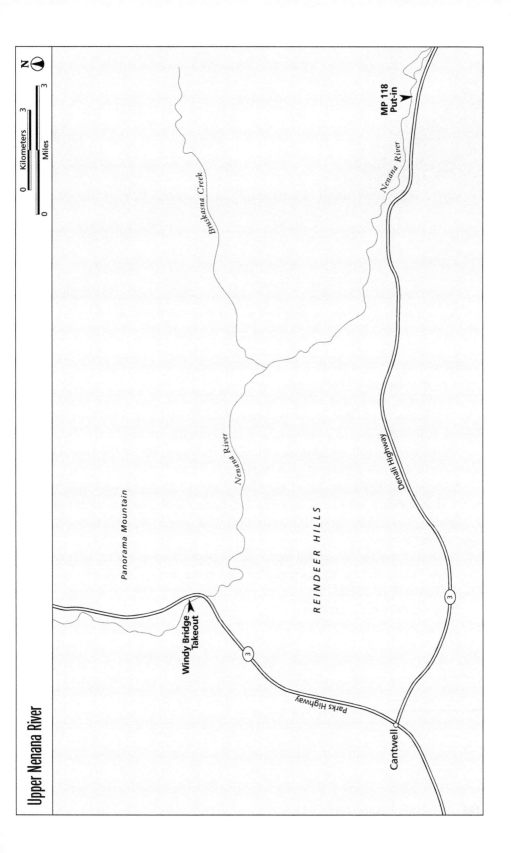

On clear days on the upper Nenana, the scenery can be a distraction from reading the water.

a problem for the river traveler as long as you stay below the high-water line where there are abundant gravel bar campsites.

The number one hazard on this float is sweepers. Most spruce-lined banks will have at least one or two leaners into the main current. A strong, alert paddler in a flat bottom boat will be able to avoid them with room to spare.

There are places with straightforward Class II chop and riffles. A few large single rocks can be found at the base of rocky bluffs.

A few notable landmarks are a large Ahtna camp on the left about 8 miles into the float. Roughly 5 miles after the camp, Bruskasna Creek comes in on the right contributing cold, clear water. Below the Bruskasna mouth, dramatic rocky bluffs hang above the water.

The end of the float is signaled by the old limestone mine in the hill in front of Panorama Mountain. Line up along the left bank when you see a homesite on the left just before Windy Bridge.

Enjoy the float. It is a great one.

36 Lower Tangle Lakes and Upper Delta River–Denali Highway to Richardson Highway Mile 212.5

Character: A clear water lake and river paddle across the tundra, with a portage and rapids section to make things interesting.

Distance: 27 miles.

Estimated paddling time: Roughly 12 hours, including the portage. Plan on 2 to 3 days total trip time.

Boat types: Plastic kayak or plastic canoe; the boat must be capable of being portaged.

Special features: Tundra, clear water, lakes, rapids, and great grayling fishing.

Difficulties: Intermediate. Class II to III rapids, portage, strong upriver winds, and braided section.

Season: Mid-June through early September.

Contact for more information: For general information, do a web search for "Bureau of Land Management Tangle Lakes Delta River."

Overview

This float across the tundra is richly varied considering it is so short: a lake paddle, portage, rapids, clear water fishing, and braided river paddling all in a compressed package. This is truly a great paddle for a long weekend.

However, the tundra is fragile. The BLM (Bureau of Land Management) recommends staying in established campsites to limit the extent of damage to the vegetation. The following campsites shown on the map, labeled A through F, are repeated here in rough GPS coordinates:

Long Tangle Lake Campsite A: N63 09323' / W145 95013'

Lower Tangle Lake Campsite B: N63 12833' / W145 95213'

Lower Tangle Lake Campsite C: N63 13952' / W145 95457'

Delta River Campsite D: N63 19882' / W145 81829'

Delta River Campsite E: N63 20114' / W145 81718'

Delta River Campsite F: N63 22383' / W145 80295'

General Access

Put-in, Tangle Lakes Campground at mile 21.3 of the Denali Highway: This campground can fill up quickly in the summer. There is a boat launch and overnight parking area.

Takeout, parking area at mile 212.5 of the Richardson Highway: The turnoff is not marked, so you need to pay close attention to the mile markers. Once below the highway, there is a BLM pamphlet stand, as well as a sign on the river warning paddlers to pull over here above Black Rapids. Be sure to walk to the river and get a

Someone probably tried to run the unrunnable falls before there was a portage trail.

These are the rapids at the base of the portage trail.

good look at the takeout since the precise location changes every year due to shifting gravel bars.

The Paddling

Set out from Tangle Lakes Campground. The boat launch is on Round Lake in a small lobe isolated from the rest of the lake.

The paddling down the chain of Round, Long, and Lower Tangle Lakes goes surprisingly quickly as long as the headwind isn't blasting—which is not always a sure thing. There is a surprisingly strong current flowing in the channels between the lake, and it even transfers to the lakes themselves sometimes. The connecting channels can be shallow, and you will probably have to drag the boat over rocks and gravel in at least a few places.

The channel narrows below Lower Tangle Lake, picks up speed, and gets rocky. The last few hundred feet before the portage could even be considered Class II. A sign appears on river-left telling you to stay river-right just above the portage trail-head. Cross to the trailhead sign on river-right and begin portaging!

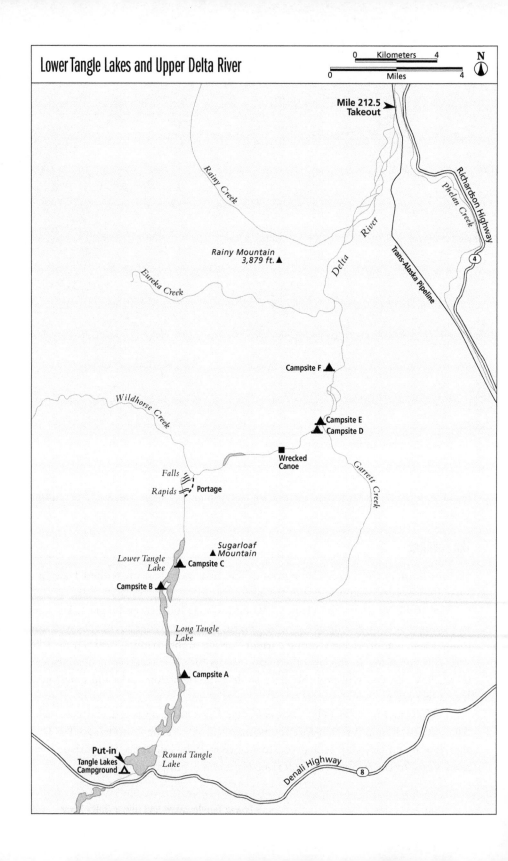

Lower Tangle Lakes and Upper Delta River

0 Kilometers 4
0 Miles 4

N

Mile 212.5
Takeout

Rainy Creek

Richardson Highway

Phelan Creek

Rainy Mountain
3,879 ft. ▲

Delta River

Eureka Creek

Trans-Alaska Pipeline

4

Campsite F ▲

Wildhorse Creek

Campsite E ▲
Campsite D ▲

■
Wrecked
Canoe

Garrett Creek

Falls
Rapids Portage

Sugarloaf
▲ Mountain
▲ Campsite C

Lower Tangle
Lake

Campsite B ▲

Long Tangle
Lake

▲ Campsite A

Put-in
Tangle Lakes
Campground △

Round Tangle
Lake

Denali Highway

8

The portage trail is steep and rocky but well maintained. There is an outhouse (with informative unpublished maps inside) roughly 100 yards down the trail from the trailhead. It is roughly 0.2 miles to a small pond. Paddle across it, then portage another 0.2 miles down a steep path to the river. This foot and paddle path sidesteps an unrunnable waterfall at the bend in the river. The BLM requests that no one camp at the portage trail to relieve pressure on the area.

The Class II to III rapids below the falls last for roughly a mile. The river is narrow, swift, and rocky. Whitewater experience is a must to safely run this section. The rapids can be a more solid Class III at high water. However, the Delta River is rain fed and regulated by lakes, so water levels do not fluctuate as rapidly and dramatically as some rain-fed Interior rivers.

The clear water continues below the rapids. A wrecked canoe is tied to a spruce tree at N63 19007' / W145 85245'. Someone probably tried to run the falls before there was a portage trail. There are few open gravel bars for camping since water levels tend to be steady. There are established camps just above Garrett Creek on the right, and a little below it on the left. Campsite F is by an abandoned cabin on an oxbow below the braided stretch after Garrett Creek. These sites are marked on this map and the GPS coordinates are given in the "Overview" section

With the addition of Eureka Creek, the Delta becomes silty, braided, and fast. It is Class II choppy water. Picking the channel can be a bit of a challenge. However, since the surrounding country is mostly tundra and there are few spruce trees, sweepers are less of a perpetual hazard than on other braided rivers. Headwinds can be challenging, though.

The Trans-Alaska pipeline almost reaches the bank just above the mouth of Phelan Creek. Phelan Creek has different-colored water than the Delta. Follow the gravelly mouth of Phelan along the right channel, and the takeout will be just after it.

37 Upper Tangle Lakes

Character: A scenic lake paddle and portage system across the tundra.

Distance: Variable. 9.5 miles from the campground to Dickey Lake.

Estimated paddling time: Variable.

Boat types: Good portaging canoe, preferably with a keel.

Special features: Portage trails, open tundra, and strong winds.

Difficulties: Advanced beginner. Class I, wind, finding the portages.

Season: Mid-June through early September.

Contact for more information: Do a web search for "Bureau of Land Management Tangle Lakes."

Overview

This gorgeous system of lakes and portage trails sits in a wide valley of open tundra. It is splendid in the fall—often particularly so around Labor Day weekend, when the

The Upper Tangle Lakes lie in a broad, tundra valley.

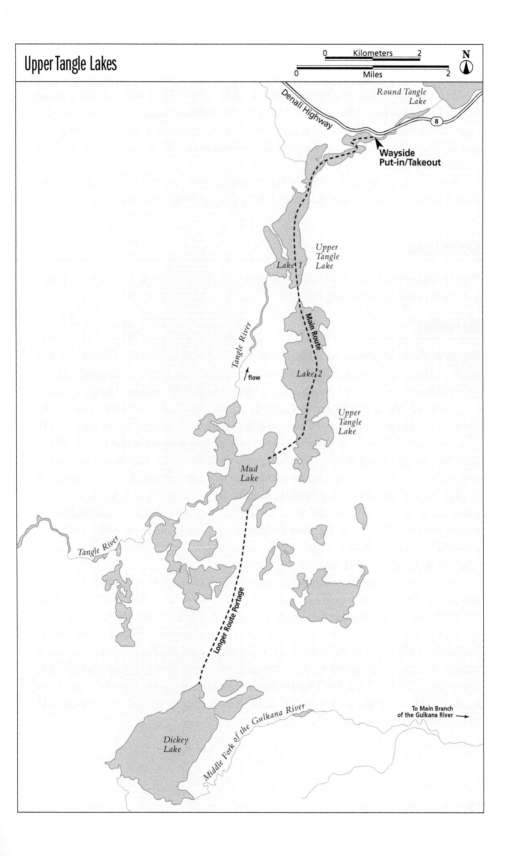

tundra is turning colors. After the second lake, portages are no longer marked and you must pick the route over the open tundra.

Wind can be a real challenge on these lakes; it rips along and can often make North Dakotans feel right at home. A light, flat-bottom canoe that is nice to portage can be impossible to control on the still water, much less make forward progress in. If you have a tailwind setting out, remember it will be much more difficult coming back.

A return trip down the Tangle River can be shallow and rocky with lots of boat dragging. Plastic boats that you don't mind getting scratched up are best for that water.

General Access

Put-in/takeout: Delta NW&SR Wayside, mile 21.7. There is a boat launch and long-term parking at this day use area.

The Paddling

Put-in at the boat launch on Lake 1. A few motorboats may be on this lake. A flat, sandy portage trail travels a half mile between Lake 1 and Lake 2. Beyond Lake 2, you will have to scout your own portages, but this is not difficult on the open tundra.

The third lake is Mud Lake (technically an unnamed lake, but called Mud Lake informally, and named for sake of clarity in this context), which is shallow and muddy. The lake is so shallow, in dry years, it is possible to drag bottom in the middle of the lake. The Tangle River flows from the northwest lobe of the lake down to Lake 1 and can make a nice return loop. However, the lake entrance to the river channel is so shallow you will always drag bottom, and the lake bottom there is just goo, so you cannot step out of the boat and push through it. You have to do a combination of body schooch and paddling through dirt to get the boat to move forward one foot at a time. The channel itself is quite shallow, and a plastic boat is almost essential since you will be bouncing and dragging over rocks.

Few people go paddle and portage south of Mud Lake. You can create your own open-ended exploration, floating and walking between the many small lakes. Past the small lakes, it is a further 1-mile-plus portage to Dickey Lake, the headwaters of the Middle Fork of the Gulkana River. There is a four-wheeler trail from the Denali Highway to Dickey Lake and there are many large campsites around the lake, so it is not as remote as the paddling and portaging effort makes it feel. The Middle Fork flows out of Dickey Lake for 24 miles before reaching the main branch of the Gulkana. The Middle Fork is swift, rocky, shallow, frequently tree- and sweeper-choked in the lower stretches, and rarely paddled.

38 Main Branch of the Gulkana River–Paxson Lake to Sourdough

Character: A varied, multiday float with many different water types and great fishing.

Distance: 47 river miles from Paxson Lake Campground to Sourdough Creek Campground.

Estimated paddling time: 2 to 4 days.

Boat types: Cataraft or plastic-hulled kayak. (Plastic-hulled, non-whitewater canoes are marginal and should only be paddled by experts.)

Special features: Broad variety of water types and strong king salmon run. Class IV Canyon Rapids has a portage trail around it, allowing experienced boaters to play in the rapids over and over again.

Difficulties: Advanced intermediate. Class II to III rock garden rapids at the Paxson Lake outlet, Class IV rapids in the canyon (with a portage trail around them), rocky Class II to III rapids below the canyon, rocks that heavily loaded boats can get repeatedly stuck on at low water, long stretches of slackwater that can be tiring to row a raft through, and bugs like you wouldn't believe.

Season: Late May through the end of September.

Contact for more information: Do a web search for "Bureau of Land Management Paxson Sourdough."

Overview

The Main Branch of the Gulkana River is one the most popular rivers in the Southern Interior to float. And for good reason. This route includes almost all types of freshwater floating: a lake paddle, Class II to III rapids, flowing streams, a portage, optional Class IV rapids, and swamp water. Grayling fishing can be so good it becomes boring to catch fish. And a strong run of king salmon also comes up this far into the Interior from the Copper River. There are abundant camping places, above and throughout the canyon, with a sod-roofed, breezy-walled cabin below the Paxson Lake outlet.

The Gulkana is primarily a snowmelt- and rain-fed flow. Water levels drop off quite a bit later in summer, and shallow draft, lightly loaded boats are a much more fun way to paddle at that time of year since it is easy to get stuck on submerged rocks. There are also many fewer people on the river, especially after the king salmon run is over.

As a last note, many families and large groups tend to float this river. Many people translates into many piles of gear. Many boats on this river are almost laughably overloaded. The laughter stops when it's time to portage around the canyon, or row the raft through the long sections of slackwater, or repeatedly push the boat off shallowly submerged rocks. A little paring of the gear before leaving will be amply rewarded by more fun on the water.

General Access

Put-in at Paxson Lake Campground: Turn west from milepost 175 on the Richardson Highway. This well-designed BLM (Bureau of Land Management) campground

This sod-roofed cabin is a popular stop, especially during nasty weather.

and boat launch is on the shores of scenic Paxson Lake. There are ample camping spots, free overnight parking, and a developed boat launch.

Takeout at Sourdough Creek Campground: Turn west at mile 147.5 into this BLM campground, boat launch, and overnight parking area.

The Paddling

From Paxson Lake Campground: Put in at the boat launch. There is a register to leave your trip information (although potentially helpful, it is optional). Special fishing regulations are also posted here.

If you are in a raft without a motor, leave as early as possible in the morning, or else late at night, to avoid contrary winds on Paxson Lake. There are a few established but informal campsites along the west lakeshore before the outlet. The hole at the outlet can have tremendous grayling fishing.

The 3 miles from the lake outlet to the Middle Fork of the Gulkana are shallow, fast, and rocky Class II and III water. Many of the rapids are rock gardens, which means you will smash into at least some rocks. A number of boats capsize on this section every year. If the water level is low and the boat loaded, you will have to get out and push frequently.

The confluence with the Middle Fork has constantly changing channels. Take the unlikely-looking, smaller one to the right to get to the established camp spot with an outhouse. Take the wider channel to the left to camp on the island. A third of a mile downstream on the left bank (N62 84045' / W145 66487') is the sod-roofed, abandoned cabin shown below. During the height of king salmon season, it will almost always be occupied.

Until the canyon, the channel is Class I and II, flowing along at most water levels pretty well, although rafters will have to row hard through some bends where the current slows. Odd boulders do pop up in the channel, but they are usually easily avoided. Grayling fishing is great through here—catching them is so easy it is a good place to introduce children to fishing.

There are numerous informal but established camping spots on this section. There is no need to create your own. Most of the camp spots are on the points of islands or on bends.

Canyon Rapids: A warning sign on the left bank clearly tells you to pull over to the left. You will already have felt the water moving faster. At higher water levels, beaching the boat can be tricky, so hustle to the bank as soon as you see the sign. There is also limited room on the bank, so be considerate of others when tying up.

The portage trail around the Class IV Canyon Rapids is well maintained and heavily traveled—the more gear you have, the more times you will walk it. The rapids can be scouted from the trail. If you are running the rapids, portage your gear to lighten the boat. The right side of the channel is the easiest route through the biggest rapids.

There are a number of well-established, heavily used campsites at the end of the portage trail with an outhouse as well. There are frequently two or more groups camping. Many people with whitewater boats set up here to run the canyon multiple times, portaging upriver on the trail, then playing in the water all day.

(*Note:* Some maps show the Haggard Creek Trail heading east from the canyon to the road. It will be some of the most brutal walking you ever do in your life. It is 5 miles of swamp and ponds torn up by four-wheelers. It takes 6 or 7 wet, mosquito-bitten hours to slog to the pull-out at milepost 161 on the Richardson Highway. If you have to bail from the canyon, take this trail. But do not lightly set out to walk it. You are in for an ordeal. If the water is unexpectedly too high and pushy to paddle, stash your boat and non-food gear in the woods by the river, battle the "trail," then return in a few weeks in another boat after the water level drops.)

The next 9 miles down from the canyon are Class II and III rapids. They are easier to negotiate than the Paxson Lake outlet but still require constant vigilance. At low and medium water levels, your boat will make frequent contact with rocks, sometimes at high speeds. This section is where the Gulkana earns its reputation as a boat destroyer. Plastic hulls are a necessity for kayaks and canoes. High-quality rafts are a must.

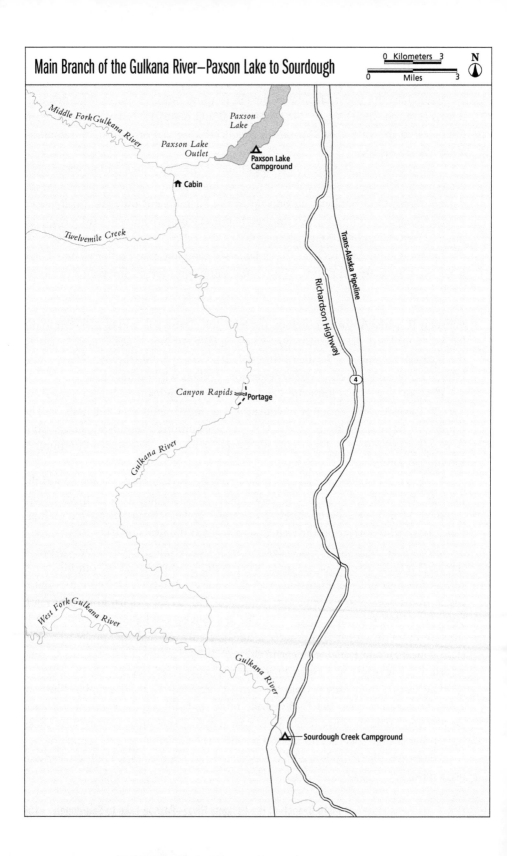

Main Branch of the Gulkana River—Paxson Lake to Sourdough

0 Kilometers 3

0 Miles 3

N

Middle Fork Gulkana River

Paxson Lake

Paxson Lake Outlet

△ Paxson Lake Campground

⌂ Cabin

Twelvemile Creek

Trans-Alaska Pipeline

Richardson Highway

4

Canyon Rapids ⇟ Portage

Gulkana River

West Fork Gulkana River

Gulkana River

△— Sourdough Creek Campground

There are plenty of excellent campsites throughout the lower canyon on the numerous gravel bars and bends. If you are expecting to camp in one spot and find it already occupied, just float on a little farther to the next spot. There is no need to crowd people.

After the canyon, the water is flat Class I. Rafters will begin rowing hard.

A mile or so above the junction with the West Fork, a sign indicates that motorboat travel is not recommended above the sign. You may see a boat or two a little above the sign, but that will be it.

At the mouth of the West Fork, motorboat traffic picks up considerably, especially during king salmon season. The mouth is quite a good hole and there will almost certainly be groups camped or anchored here.

Motorboats, for the most part, are quite courteous to paddlers on this river and almost always think about their wake and reduce its effect on you. Return the favor and give them the deep channel if you can.

After passing underneath the Trans-Alaska pipeline, Sourdough Creek Campground is unmistakably on the left.

39 Little Nelchina River to Nelchina River to Tazlina Lake to Tazlina River

Character: A multiday whitewater run down glacial rivers, with a lake float in the middle.
Distance: 74 miles total, including an 8-mile lake crossing.
Estimated paddling time: Approximately 20 cumulative hours. Allow at least 3 to 4 days total trip time.
Boat types: Cataraft or river kayak.
Special features: Glacial outflow, large lake, lots of rapids, fast water, and great scenery.
Difficulties: Expert. Furthermore, this river should only be floated by experienced Alaska river paddlers. Almost continuous Class II, with random Class III sections. Two Class III to IV rapids. Narrow Little Nelchina River has lots of sweepers, swift water, rocks, and shallow sections. A long lake crossing in the middle of the trip can be a further challenge. There are no takeouts mid-trip.
Season: Mid-June through early September. The end of June and beginning of July is the height of the floating season on these rivers with highly variable water flow.
Contact for more information: No contacts for this route.

Overview

This trip provides days of fast floating, with a wide variety of water types along the way. Distant snow-covered peaks from the Wrangell–St. Elias Range frame the surrounding hills. The Tazlina Glacier flows into Tazlina Lake. The scenery gazing from the boat is something else.

The Little Nelchina is a narrow, shallow, rain-fed creek. There are lots of sweepers, some fast water, many shallow sections, and rocks in the channel to get a big raft hung up on. The Nelchina River itself is glacier fed. It is fast, with random boulders in the channel. The Tazlina Lake basin is filled with meltwater from retreating Tazlina Glacier. It is a roughly 8-mile float from the Nelchina River delta across the lake to the outlet. Powerful, cold winds form on the glacier and rip across the lake. Rafters in particular should be prepared to camp on the lake for at least a few days waiting out wind and waves. Almost all rafters bring small motors for the lake crossing. The Tazlina River itself is extremely fast, with two major rapids, and almost continuous Class II rapids, with random boulders and Class III rapids, which require constant vigilance and steering. All of these conditions are radically affected by changing water levels and year-to-year channel changes. Expect to do original navigation at all times.

Once starting this trip, you are committed to the next 74 miles. Although the Glenn Highway roughly parallels this route to the north, it would be a brutal walk through swamps to reach it and should only be attempted under extraordinary, emergency circumstances. Water levels fluctuate dramatically, and any paddler attempting this route must be prepared for the full range of possible conditions along the way. The water level at the put-in on the rain-fed Little Nelchina is not necessarily predicative of what water levels will be like on the Nelchina and Tazlina Rivers since those rivers are glacier meltwater fed. If it has been hot and dry, the Little Nelchina can be low and the Nelchina and Tazlina high, swift, and extremely pushy with large waves. Or vice versa if it has been rainy and cool. Some years, a glacial dam in the headwaters of the Nelchina River breaks, unleashing a flash flood. There is no way to predict when this will happen.

A roughly 12-foot cataraft with a flow-through floor, motor mount, and small motor is the approximately ideal craft for the range of possible conditions. One raft in the party can have a motor and tow a train of rafts across the lake. There are reports of some rafts using sails for the lake crossing, but do not count on favorable winds.

This trip will certainly require the active participation of passengers on rafts, either by shifting their weight, pushing through shallows, spotting rocks while the rower is spotting sweepers, or by pushing a hung-up raft off a boulder in moving water. All people should be dressed—at least with neoprene waders—for standing in frigid water. This is not a good trip for one expert rafter to bring a lot of novices along in the boat.

All that said, this trip is almost unique in that it provides days of fast water, mind-blowing scenery, great camping spots, and isolation, all with relatively easy road access. This is truly a memorable float.

General Access

Put-in, Little Nelchina River, mile 137.6 on the Glenn Highway: The turnoff is not signed, but is on the east side of the Little Nelchina Bridge. Nominally a state campground, the put-in is not staffed or maintained. Although I have never heard reports of vandalism there, it is not a serene spot to leave a vehicle unattended for long periods of time, so, try to avoid leaving a vehicle there if at all possible. Allow 6 hours to set up the car shuttle if starting from Anchorage.

Takeout, mile 110.6 on the Richardson Highway: This day use and parking area on the southeast corner of the Tazlina Bridge used to be a heavily used fishing spot but is now closed to fishing due to bank erosion. The boat launch is next to the bridge.

The Paddling

Little Nelchina River: The water typically has a greenish tinge but turns brown and rises quickly after heavy rains. If the water level feels too high standing at the put-in on the Little Nelchina, either find another trip to do or wait a few days for the level to subside.

The Little Nelchina lives up to its name: narrow and shallow. It is also fast. There are many, many sweepers along shore, and constant hard rowing and steering will be a necessity. Boats will almost certainly get stuck in shallows requiring pushing, especially at the beginning. There are many riffles and rocky Class II and III rapids on this

This view of the Outlet Rapids from Tazlina Lake is looking upriver, from the left side of the wave train. There is a good scouting location just above the rapids, at the low gravel bar on the right of this picture.

section. Sometimes you will have to choose between dragging the boat and following the channel through sweepers. Always choose dragging the boat. As long as there isn't too much pushing, it takes roughly 2 hours to float the approximately 4 miles to the main Nelchina River.

Nelchina River: The Nelchina River is fed by meltwater from the Nelchina Glacier. The water is fast, gray, and silty. By the middle of summer, it is semi-continuous Class II rapids, with occasional and random Class III patches. Watch for random boulders in the channel; rocks are very hard to spot in the muddy water. There are numerous possible camp spots along the sand and gravel banks. The Nelchina begins to braid roughly 4 to 5 miles above Tazlina Lake. The main channel is not difficult to follow by braided river standards, but you can fight a cold, strong headwind coming off the glacier in the afternoons and evenings.

Tazlina Lake: It works best to begin a lake crossing in the early morning before the wind picks up. Therefore, many groups make camp in the evening at the mouth of Mendeltna Creek, near the Nelchina delta, before crossing the lake in the morning. There are some private cabins on the north side of the Mendeltna mouth, but they are rarely occupied. Please respect private property. Most groups camp below the

Little Nelchina River to Nelchina River to Tazlina Lake to Tazlina River

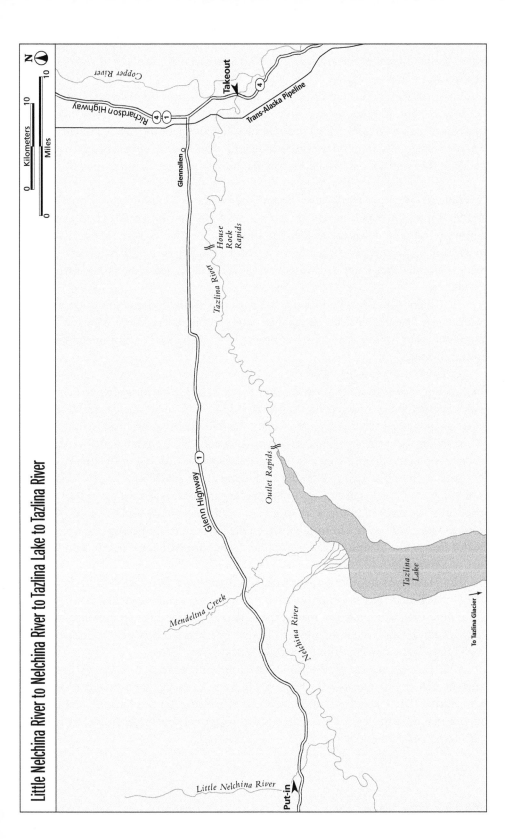

water line just south of the creek mouth. This area is also the focus of glacial winds, so dress warm and windproof.

A lake crossing with a raft and 2- or 3-horsepower motor should proceed at 2 or so miles an hour, assuming there aren't contrary winds. Always pack extra days' food in case you wind up camping a long time on the lake waiting for the weather to change. Do not stray too far from shore while crossing the lake since the weather can change suddenly. The north shore has, almost continuously, good potential camp spots.

Tazlina River: A gravel spit at the Tazlina Lake outlet is an ideal place to scout the Outlet Rapids. The rapids are, at most water levels, Class III, with a train of large standing waves running down the middle and strong back eddies along both banks. The right bank has large rocks within the waves. I have run the wave train on the left side without trouble, but scout and make your own decisions according to the specific conditions.

The Tazlina River is swift. Like the Nelchina, it is semi-continuous Class II water, with random patches of Class III standing waves and boulders. However, below the outlet the water is clear with a green tinge, so it is much easier to spot the boulders in the channel.

Although the entire channel is fast and a little rough, requiring constant vigilance, there is one more major set of rapids. After floating the Tazlina for approximately 21 miles, the channel narrows, picks up speed, and becomes more boulder filled, with snag mounds along shore. After a few bends, the river makes a hard right. At the top of the rapids, there are large boulders on the left bank, with powerful pour-overs and deep holes behind them. Swing a little right to avoid them. But just below these rocks is a large rock on the right, House Rock, located at N62 083789' / W145 766287' and visible on Google Earth. The current will try to drive your boat either into the rock or to the right of it. You want to go left of the rock. In all likelihood, you will have to pull hard and fast to make it. (It is called House Rock because, supposedly, with a heavy dose of artistic license, it appears house shaped. However, it is about the size of a Volkswagen.)

The Tazlina will be at least a 1 or 2 miles an hour faster than the Nelchina below the Outlet Rapids, and it gathers speed as it flows along, finishing around 2 miles or so an hour faster at the takeout than at the outlet. The water also becomes siltier and grayer with distance, acquiring more silt every time it passes beneath the numerous high bluffs. The 42 miles of the Tazlina pass quickly.

After passing underneath the Trans-Alaska pipeline, it is another 4 miles to the takeout. When you spot the Richardson Highway bridge, pull to the right bank immediately. The takeout is immediately after the bridge, so you must be within a foot or two of shore as you pass underneath it. If you miss the bridge, it is extremely difficult to pull farther down.

40 Copper River–Chitina to Cordova

Character: A fast, wide glacial river with spectacular scenery and wildlife.

Distance: 85 miles from Chitina to the Million Dollar Bridge, a further 23 miles from the bridge to Flag Point.

Estimated paddling time: 4 days from Chitina to the Million Dollar Bridge, 1 additional day to Flag Point.

Boat types: Cataraft.

Special features: Towering mountains, glaciers entering the river, fast current, unusual wildlife, historic railroad ruins, and hiking trails leading from the river.

Difficulties: Expert. Furthermore, this river should only be floated by experienced Alaska river paddlers. Class I to III, 7 to 9 miles per hour average current, whirlpools, powerful eddies, upriver wind, dust storms, high bear density at rapids, icebergs, and no mid-trip takeouts.

Season: June through September.

Contact for more information: For general land management information, do a web search for "Chugach National Forest Cordova" and "Wrangell-St. Elias National Park Copper River."

Overview

The Copper River has the most spectacular scenery of any paddle in this book. It is, arguably, the most gorgeous float in the state. Peaks up to 7,000 feet high line the bank. Glaciers calve directly into the channel. Seals follow the salmon runs inland 50 miles from the ocean. Brown bears troll the rapids for salmon, in a less publicized, but no less dramatic, concentration than the more famous McNeil River or Brooks Falls areas. The abandoned Copper River and Northwestern Railroad grade follows the right bank, with ruins and tunnels to explore. A number of trailheads begin at the river and lead inland to glaciers and open ridges. This float is truly unique.

A Copper River journey demands previous experience with Alaska conditions. It is not the place to learn how to do things. The current rips along at an average 7 to 9 miles per hour at routine water levels, and up to twice as fast through canyons and rapids. Boiling eddies and boat-grabbing whirlpools form along rock walls lining the river. The silt load is so heavy that the grains will rasp against the boat hull, sounding like sandpaper being continuously rubbed against the boat. The flowing water was ice not too long ago, as the glaciers hanging onto the peaks above the river constantly remind you. Flipping the boat, in all likelihood, would be fatal. Crossing the river can take a long, long time, and can even be impossible in contrary currents. A cataraft or a doughnut raft with a rowing frame are by far the most stable crafts for this trip.

Strong winds blast upriver, presenting an almost constant headwind. The current in most sections is strong enough you can paddle against the wind, even in a cataraft. But there are sections of slackwater and a lake where it is all but impossible to fight the wind in a raft. Furthermore, the enormous bare sand dunes of the Bremner Flats routinely get worked into dust storms so thick that a Dust Bowl farmer of the 1930s would find the conditions familiar. The wind tends to get strongest in the hot

Brown bears fish the Abercrombie Rapids. It can be more dangerous to scout the rapids than to run them.

afternoon and die down late at night until early in the morning. This is not a trip for people who like to sleep in since you will almost certainly have to get up early—sometimes even 3 or 4 in the morning—to paddle while the wind is still calm. Since it is so difficult to paddle in the afternoon and evening, the paddling day is limited, and you cannot count on paddling long hours if you really need to make miles.

This is a glacial river, and it has counterintuitive flow dynamics compared to rain-fed or snowmelt-fed rivers. The hotter and drier it gets, the more the river rises as the tributary glaciers melt. On hot days, this means that gravel bars in the middle of the river can be exposed early in the afternoon but underwater by evening. This is the only river in this book where camping on mid-river gravel bars is not recommended. Instead, camp high on the gravel mouths of tributaries, which also frequently have clear water for drinking and cooking. Set a vertical stick in the mud at the water level when you beach for the evening. This will give a sense of the rate of water rise or drop over the course of the night so you can position boats, gear, and tents accordingly. But it is only a sense since the rate or even direction can change at any time.

Once you start paddling, you are committed to the trip; after passing the mouth of O'Brien Creek 4 miles from the put-in, there are no places to pull out for the next 80 miles. If water levels rise unexpectedly to flood stage, you have to paddle through to the end of the trip or camp for days, waiting for conditions to change. Winds don't always die down at night, and getting pinned down in camp for days at a stretch is relatively common. *Always bring at least a few days' extra food.* A stack of books is also handy for quality camping time.

It gets colder on the Copper River than most people expect. The constant upriver wind forms over the cool water of Prince William Sound and glacial ice. A good windbreaker, warm layered clothes, a windproof musher's hat, and neoprene gloves will make the trip much happier. Commercial fishing–quality rain wear is also essential.

All that said, the Copper River can be the best float of your life. The conditions that require experience and thought while planning and paddling make for a unique journey you will fondly tell stories about for years to come.

General Access

Put-in, Copper River Bridge at Chitina, mile 1.3 on the McCarthy Road: Drive through the town of Chitina, through the one-lane railroad cut, cross the bridge, and take a left onto the unimproved gravel bars. This is the boat launch and fish wheel area. Although unimproved, the gravel bars make a natural boat launch for trailered boats. Be sure to park vehicles high enough and far enough away from the river to account for dramatically rising water levels.

Takeout, Flag Point, river mile 107: The unimproved takeout is on river-right by the microwave reflector tower, just before the bridge at mile 23 on the Copper River Highway.

Shuttle Discussion

The vehicle shuttle makes this a tough trip to do. The put-in at Chitina is at the end of the Edgerton Highway, off the Richardson Highway. It is a roughly 6-hour drive from Anchorage, or 7 from Fairbanks, not including road construction delays. It works best to drive your own vehicle there.

Retrieving the vehicle from the put-in is a little tricky. The easiest way to get it back is to convince some friends to go to Chitina with you, perhaps taking in a little dipnetting or a jaunt to Kennicott while they are at it, and then driving your vehicle back. (And it works even better if they meet you at the ferry dock in Whittier on the return leg.)

Make arrangements prior to leaving to get picked up on the Copper River Highway at Flag Point. Beyond Flag Point there is not road access due to a bridge failure on the Copper River Highway. Cordova Coastal Outfitters (www.cdvcoastal.com) has done pickups in the past. You will have to specify a date and time and pickup location. Make sure that they will store your gear overnight and give you a ride to the ferry. The ferry now leaves Cordova daily. You will have to find an empty van or truck to carry your gear prior to boarding since the ferry does not want you making multiple loading trips with loose gear. It is best if your shuttle drivers help you with this since they know people in town. Discuss all these points on the telephone when planning.

The ferry goes from Cordova to Valdez or Whittier. You will have to make further arrangements from there. However, if taking the train from Whittier to Anchorage, check and be sure of the arrival time in Anchorage since it may be a tourist excursion train.

The Paddling

Copper River Bridge, put-in mile 0: Remember to park your vehicle high enough on the gravel bar to account for water level fluctuations.

The float underneath the bridge and around the turn past the wide mouth of the Chitina River is an introduction to paddling on a big glacial river. The river will feel big and probably a little intimidating. It will likely be windy, especially in the afternoon and evening. Swing wide of the strong eddy at the rocky point on the right shore as you make the right turn after the bridge. From here to the mouth, the strongest eddies and whirlpools will be along the rocky bluffs on shore. Stay away from them. (This and one other large, strong eddy is marked on this map, but there are, at the very least, hundreds more on the river. They vary in size and location according to water levels, shifting currents, erosion, and so on. *You have to use your own judgment to avoid them.*)

Mile 4: A drivable road extends as far as the mouth of O'Brien Creek on the right bank. The road is no longer maintained formally past the creek, and landslides have rendered it impassable in a vehicle. There has been a lot of disputes over land at the mouth of O'Brien Creek and, as of this writing, boat landing is not allowed here. It was used for years as the landing for dipnetters, and older guidebooks may mark this as a put-in. For the foreseeable future, it should only be used in an emergency. It is the last road-accessible point on the river before the takeouts.

Mile 6: Shortly after the mouth of Taral Creek, you float into Wood Canyon. There may be many dipnetters on the rocks through here. Dipnetting is permitted for Alaska residents from the Copper River Bridge through Woods Canyon, as far as the orange signs just above Haley and Canyon Creeks. The water boils strongly and variably along the canyon walls. The current rips right through here, with tremendous random boils, whirlpools, and a few standing waves. Stick to the middle of the river to avoid the strongest eddies along the walls of both sides of the canyon. The rocky points sticking out from the walls tend to create the strongest, largest eddies.

Mile 10: At the end of Wood Canyon, the river widens, and you will probably see the orange signs on the right and left banks above Canyon and Haley Creeks. These mark the end of the dipnetting area. *Immediately upon exiting, pull hard to the left bank, toward the mouth of Canyon Creek.* The rocky headland that juts into the right side of the river, just below the mouth of Haley Creek, creates the Headwall Eddy (also sometimes called the Haley Creek Eddy) at the end of the point. This has huge, random whirlpools and powerful upriver, boiling currents. You do not want to get sucked into it. It is very difficult to get out of and could flip the boat. I have heard rumors of the eddy reaching almost over to the left bank but have not personally seen that happen. Pull hard to the left bank as soon as the river widens at the end of the canyon, then stick to the left bank well past the headland point, and the eddy should be avoidable.

(*Note*: United States Geological Survey maps show Wood Canyon beginning just above Tenas Creek and extending another 2 miles below the Headwall Eddy. But, for all practical purposes, and the way it is referred to by heavy users of the river as well as this guide, Wood Canyon begins just past Taral Creek and ends just above Haley and Canyon Creeks.)

Miles 10 to 50: The river widens and still flows along quickly after the canyon but is no longer as boiling. Strong eddies still form along the shore, however, particularly around rocky points. Almost any decent size creek flowing into the river will have a sand or gravel mouth, which makes a nice camping spot. Most of the small tributaries have clear water. If you do camp by muddy water, boil it and then let it sit overnight. The silt will have settled by morning and you can pour (reasonably) clear water off the top, discarding most of the silt.

The former Copper River and Northwestern Railroad grade, tunnels, and rotting trestles line the right bank and, once you leave the canyon, may make tempting stops. A number of people report exploring the tunnels and even camping in them. I have not been able to find a tunnel visible from the river that didn't have strong eddies along the shore preventing a safe landing.

Although there are numerous potential camp spots at creek mouths all along the river, the informal Waterfall camp spot (N61 14718' / W144 89782') is marked on this map. Suitable for small groups up to around six people and up to two large boats, it has the unusual advantage of being surrounded by high rocky walls, which makes it very unlikely to be visited by bears. There is also a lovely waterfall with clear water.

The Bremner Flats are roughly 20 square miles of bare sand and silt exposed to winds focused by converging valleys. By afternoon, the blowing silt can fill the entire valley for miles upriver. The mouth of Cleave Creek and sandbars on the left shore just below Cleave are frequently the last dust-free camping spots above the Flats. If it is afternoon, you may have to camp here, waiting for the next morning for the wind to die. It is possible to have to wait multiple days here.

Miles 50 to 70: As you begin paddling toward the Flats, preferably early in the morning when the wind is calm, stick to the right bank, even through the confusing gravel bars of the Tasnuna River mouth. You don't want to get too far river-left near the exposed bars because the water is shallowest and slowest there. It can be challenging to row a raft into a headwind as the current slows around the Flats. But, after passing the mouth of the unnamed Sheils Glacier outlet creek, also the trailhead for the Sheils Glacier Trail (N60 87944' / W144 66274'), you will be along the lee shore and upwind of blowing silt.

There are a few campsites on the left shore above Baird Canyon, especially at the mouth of the Wernicke River. There is a trailhead here, as well. It can be a hard paddle to cross from the right shore to left, across the current. But, it will probably work out best to camp here, so you can paddle Baird Canyon, Abercrombie Rapids, and Miles Lake in the morning.

(*Note about trailheads:* This is a paddling guide, and hiking trails are beyond the scope of these pages. I have not walked them far myself. However, I have heard reports that they have more in common with bushwhacking than a stroll on a walking trail. The routes are, theoretically, blazed with orange diamond reflectors. The USDA Forest Service has also posted white signs, easily seen from the river, declaring public easements at the trailheads. This is because the trails start from, then cross Alaska Native corporation land. The easements permit only 24 hours of camping and walking through on the trail. If you plan on hiking, think about how to store unattended food near the river.)

Below the Wernicke River, Baird Fish Camp appears on the right. It is the camp for people tending the fish wheels in Baird Canyon. Just below the camp is another trailhead on the left.

Miles 70 to 75: The water of Baird Canyon, although fast, has fewer boils and eddies than the upriver Wood Canyon. Stay away from the rocky shores, though.

As the river widens after the canyon, stick to the right bank even though it is a longer and slower route than following the left bank. This is very important. By following

The silhouette of the Million Dollar Bridge stands out in contrast to the Childs Glacier.

the right bank, you will be lined up to beach your boat at the point above Abercrombie Rapids to scout them. If you follow the left and begin to cut right just above the rapids, strong converging currents will push you to the left, you will probably not be able to cross the river to scout, and you will have to run the rapids by the seat of your pants.

Miles 75 to 76: Abercrombie Rapids are, at most flow levels, Class III. There are relatively few rocks in the channel, but a tremendous amount of water is forced through this narrow neck. Current speeds of 20 miles per hour occur every summer. A wave train runs down the left side, with standing waves typically up to 10 feet tall. The waves look smaller from shore than they feel while running them. The waves, however, can be fun to run in a raft, but the majority of boats stick to the right where the water is smoother. This is fine, except, as soon as you pass the wave train, cut to

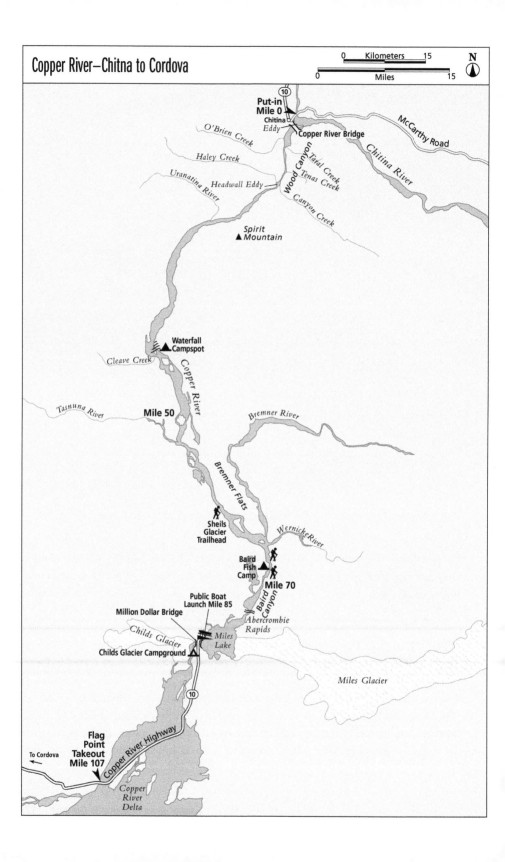

Copper River–Chitna to Cordova

0   Kilometers   15
0   Miles   15

N

Put-in
Mile 0
10
Chitina
Eddy
Copper River Bridge
McCarthy Road

O'Brien Creek
Haley Creek
Uranatina River
Headwall Eddy
Wood Canyon
Tatal Creek
Tenas Creek
Canyon Creek
Chitina River

Spirit
▲ Mountain

Waterfall
▲ Campspot
Cleave Creek
Copper River

Tasnuna River
Mile 50
Bremner River

Bremner Flats

Sheils
Glacier
Trailhead
Wernicke River

Baird
Fish
Camp
Mile 70
Baird Canyon

Public Boat
Launch Mile 85
Abercrombie
Rapids
Million Dollar Bridge
Childs Glacier
Miles
Lake
Childs Glacier Campground
10

Miles Glacier

Flag
Point
Takeout
Mile 107
To Cordova
Copper River Highway

Copper
River
Delta

river-left to avoid the hole and whirlpool on the lower right outlet of the rapids, formed by the rocky headwall at the beginning of Miles Lake.

Abercrombie Rapids can be as tricky to scout as they are to run. Salmon are concentrated in the channel and are thrown helplessly around in the current. Brown bears congregate on the right shore for the feast. They may be fishing in the water or wandering along shore. If so, make it a fast, short scout. Walk around with bear spray even if you don't see any bears when landing. Don't go into the brush to heed nature's call; modesty has its place, but this is not it.

Miles 77 to 85: Follow the left side of Miles Lake. Although technically a lake, this is where the strongest current is and sandbars fill the right side. With no wind, a cataraft can make the roughly 7-mile crossing in 2 hours. With a headwind, it can be a real struggle. There are few camping places on the lake. After passing Miles Glacier, ice chunks will float along in the lake, too. Don't get too close, since they may get upended as they ground, suddenly tripling in size.

Mile 85: The current quickly gains strength as the channel narrows before the Million Dollar Bridge. To beach the boats, cut to river-right just above the narrowing channel. The public boat launch is the gravel spot just before the bridge on river-right (N60 67525' / W144 74467').

In an emergency, the left bank just upriver of the bridge works as a landing, if you don't mind a short, steep walk up to the road.

The Childs Glacier Campground, operated by Chugach National Forest, is on the left side of the bridge, to the west of the Copper River Highway. The Copper River Highway is closed due to a bridge failure and unlikely to reopen anytime soon. There is no road access to the campground now. However, the campground is still technically open if you choose to camp there.

The campground has overnight camp spots and, crucially, benches right on the riverbank to watch the calving Childs Glacier. You will probably have heard the steady booms while crossing Miles Lake. They are truly spectacular to watch.

Mile 85 to 107: It is another short day's float past the Million Dollar Bridge to Flag Point.

The calving face of Childs Glacier just after the bridge is a serious hazard. You will want to scout the face of the glacier, either from the bridge or the campground viewing area, to check for large chunks of ice just about to break free. Theoretically, passing by the glacier in the cool of the late night will reduce the chances of calving while you paddle. But a scout or night scramble does not guarantee safety. Crashing ice chunks big enough to send waves reaching the left bank happen a dozen times a summer. There is a one in forty to fifty chance every year that a wave will overwhelm the campground itself. Paddling by the face of this glacier is just a roll of the dice. "Do I feel lucky?" is the question to ask before pushing off.

Stick to the left bank, about 100 feet or so off shore while passing the glacier. If waves do come toward you, turn your bow into the wave and paddle hard. The waves will, in all likelihood, be breaking and carrying ice, trees, and other debris.

Past the glacier, the Copper River begins to braid into many fine channels. Always stick to the right channel. You may even see low bridges off to the left, but stay to the right. The takeout is at the Flag Point Bridge, mile 23 of the Copper River Highway, a mile past high mountains that line the river. It is an unimproved, unofficial takeout on river-right, just before the bridge (N60 44644' / W145 08546'). A microwave reflector tower marks the spot. There are no facilities or phone here.

Appendix A: General Alaska Paddling Information

Paddling Clubs

Joining a paddling club is one of the best ways of meeting like-minded people, finding information about paddling routes, or picking up new skills.

In Anchorage, the Knik Canoers and Kayakers Club is active year round. They maintain a Facebook page as their primary point of contact.

In Fairbanks, the Fairbanks Paddlers Club has a large membership. Their website is www.fairbankspaddlers.org, and they have an active mailing list.

River Gauges

The National Oceanic and Atmospheric Administration Alaska-Pacific River Forecast Center has river flow gauges updated on the web in real time. These gauges are throughout the state. Do a web search for "NOAA Alaska river levels." The United States Geological Survey also operates their own set of river gauges. Do a web search for "USGS Alaska river levels" to find those.

Roads

The Milepost has mile-by-mile descriptions of roads throughout Alaska and Northwestern Canada, as well as many ads. The book is updated and published yearly and, in many ways, is more detailed than Google Maps. The annual purchase price is more than repaid in gas savings by preventing aimless wandering in a vehicle.

Appendix B: Suggested Packing List

The following packing list works well for trips longer than 3 or more days. For shorter trips, it can be pared slightly, but not by much. These lists do not include specialized gear such as waders, throw ropes, or dry suits, which may be necessary on some floats.

- ☐ sleeping bag, polyester and rated to at least 0 degrees Fahrenheit
- ☐ sleeping pad
- ☐ books, pen, journal
- ☐ headlamp and batteries
- ☐ maps
- ☐ windproof hooded jacket
- ☐ thick sweater
- ☐ 2 pairs of heavy polyester long johns
- ☐ nylon shorts
- ☐ nylon pants
- ☐ neoprene gloves
- ☐ musher's hat
- ☐ 2 pairs of warm socks
- ☐ long sleeve light shirt, polyester
- ☐ Xtra-tuff boots
- ☐ sunglasses
- ☐ ball cap
- ☐ tent repair kit
- ☐ boat repair kit
- ☐ dry bag repair kit
- ☐ duct tape
- ☐ extra rope
- ☐ food, including at least 2 to 3 days extra
- ☐ gasoline stove
- ☐ stove fuel
- ☐ pot

- ❏ bowl
- ❏ spoon
- ❏ cup
- ❏ Leatherman, or other brand multitool with pliers, wire cutters, multiple screw-driver types, and knife
- ❏ unscented soap
- ❏ bear deterrent
- ❏ camera
- ❏ wallet
- ❏ toilet paper
- ❏ first-aid kit
- ❏ extra paddle
- ❏ life jacket
- ❏ tent and ground cloth
- ❏ thermos
- ❏ water jugs
- ❏ water purification method
- ❏ rain suit
- ❏ waterproof map case
- ❏ copy of *Paddling Alaska*

Index

About the Author

Dan Maclean has been paddling Alaska for twenty-five years. He spent five summers solo canoeing the five longest rivers in Alaska from beginning to end, which he wrote about in *Paddling the Yukon River and its Tributaries*. It is the only guide to paddling the entire 2,000 miles of the Yukon River and a finalist for the Independent Publishers Book Award in 2006. Dan is a high school science teacher and lives with his family in Anchorage.